About *Play is the Way*

In years to come, when Scotland considers with pride its early years approach, we will point to this book to understand how we achieved it.

Jackie Brock, CEO, Children in Scotland

This highly readable concise wee book offers fourteen different informed perspectives on the damage done to Scots kids by missing out on play during the early years. It's a brilliant exercise in blended learning about the subject – with engaging stories, sharp science and critical analysis all in one short volume. Essential reading for anyone involved in play, education or government.

Lesley Riddoch, radio broadcaster, journalist, author, Fife

There is no doubt that play is crucial in early years settings and beyond. Any school leader, practitioner, parent or politician struggling to understand why play is so important should read this book.

George Gilchrist, former head teacher, author of 'Practitioner Enquiry', Scottish Borders

Play is the Way is a vital manual for any parent and all parents, and all school teachers. It belongs on the shelves at home and at school, not to be gathering dust but to be read and read again and, above all, to be implemented. It is a book that shapes the future for all of us, an inspired compendium of thoughtful study, common sense and practical wisdom for a better world.

Sir John Lister-Kaye OBE, naturalist and author, Scottish Highlands

Play is the Way provides a range of stimulating narratives to engage practitioners, and provocative arguments that should inform Scottish education policy development. Outdoor play brings specific benefits in health and well-being vital to childhood development, and similarly time in and with nature is vital to developing positive attitudes to sustainability. These too are strong themes of this book, and I thoroughly recommend it to anyone interested in early learning and the primary years.

Peter Higgins, Professor of Outdoor, Environmental & Sustainability Education, Edinburgh

Play is the Way . . . to a future of hope! This compact, accessible volume opens the window on a new, positive future for upcoming generations of children, and represents an opportunity to revive and transform Scotland's reputation as an educational innovator. If we want to 'Realise the Ambition' and build a community of active, creative, inventive and adaptive citizens who are equipped to embrace the opportunities and challenges of the 21st century, we need bold, courageous leaders who are willing to try something different and fly the flag for play.

Julia Whitaker, registered Health Play Specialist, Edinburgh

An important, accessible resource for practitioners, policy makers, academics and students who share an interest in early childhood. This well-composed book provides coverage of a number of vital issues, including the critical importance of play-based pedagogical practice in both early learning childcare settings and beyond. It explores the tensions between the value of rich outdoor experiences and the pressures on children for early academic achievement. It also celebrates the prominence of practitioners as researchers.

Richard Andrew, Professor of Education, Univ. of Edinburgh

Education has been re-philosophising what it is about for some time, some of that has seen shifts but there is still work to do. The Upstart Scotland campaign has led the charge to promote play-based learning in the early years. Upstart's championing at practice and policy level is now augmented with its success in drawing together a rich tapestry and kernel of knowledge. The timing of *Play is the Way*'s release could not be more apt – we are in an era where education and indeed society is asking questions about what it means to be human.

Neil McLennan, Senior Lecturer/Director of Leadership Programmes, University of Aberdeen

A wonderful book. The different viewpoints, leading the same way, give such strength and power. All early years provision must be 'rights-focused, relationship-centred and play-based'. A must read!

Victoria Lungu, Reggio Emilia atelierista

Play is the Way presents a policy to support Scotland's young children for lifetimes of well-being. It celebrates every three- to seven-year-old's hope for sharing joy of life outdoors in playful affection with loved ones. Belief that the affections and skills of free play in natural and cultural worlds is the foundation of the most sophisticated arts and science is supported by psycho-biological science of early years. Description of how intelligent knowledge and skills mature in human bodies and minds from before birth to seven or eight years in every human society reveals innate measures of 'musicality' in movement-with-feelings by which sharing of ideas and actions are both enjoyable and creative.

From before birth, a human social life benefits from exploring experiences with others in playful imagination of body movement, seeking and sharing fun in discovery. That is how we build and recall stories to tell lifetimes and centuries of 'common sense'. It is a mistake to believe that learning in education can only result from an intelligent imitation wanting to know and name seriously a teacher's facts and skills.

Colwyn Trevarthen, Professor of Child Psychology
and Psychobiology, Edinburgh

Play is the Way

Child development, early years and the future of Scottish education

Sue Palmer (Editor)

C|C|W|B press

First published by CCWB Press in 2020
Centre for Confidence and Well-being.
Registered Office Abercorn House,
79 Renfrew Rd, Paisley, PA3 4DA

Printed 2020, (twice)

**A catalogue record of this book is available
from the British Library**
978-1-91600941 1 7

Printed and bound in Great Britain by
Bell & Bain Ltd, Glasgow.

POSTCARDS FROM SCOTLAND

Series editor: Carol Craig

Advisory group:
Professor Phil Hanlon, Chair,
Centre for Confidence and Well-being;
Fred Shedden

Contents

Introduction: Why Upstart ... and where next?

Sue Palmer

As Chair of Upstart Scotland, I was delighted when *Postcards from Scotland* invited me to edit a book on early childhood education and care (ECEC). 'Early years' has always been the Cinderella of the education system, its significance for the overall success of *Curriculum for Excellence* seriously under-estimated. So I leapt at the opportunity to explain how a coherent approach to early years – centred on positive relationships and play – will not only result in improved educational performance but also in greatly improved health and well-being for future Scottish citizens.

I invited a wide range of experts to contribute chapters from their own personal and professional perspective and was thrilled at their enthusiastic response. The result is a fascinating collection of voices, making a powerful case for relationship-centred, play-based ECEC for children between three and seven years old, and showing how Upstart's dream of a 'kindergarten stage' can be achieved. The Upstart campaign is deeply grateful to all the authors for their contributions and also to Falkirk Council for allowing us to use their 'Play is the Way' slogan for our title.

The story so far. . .
In the spring of 2015, a group of people from early years, primary

education, social work and the play sector met in an Edinburgh tenement flat. All were worried about the steady increase of physical and mental health problems among children and young people – and all believed it was linked to the decline of active, self-directed, outdoor play during early childhood. Out of this meeting came Upstart Scotland – a campaign for a play-based kindergarten stage, based on the Nordic model, for Scottish children aged between three and seven. We set up a website, explaining our aims and the evidence to support them, and became active on social media.

By the time Upstart was officially launched in May 2016, the movement had gathered many thousands of supporters from all over the country. We'd set up eleven local networks, ranging from Shetland in the north to Dumfries in the south, Inverclyde in the west to Dundee in the east. Guests at the launch party included representatives not only from early years, education, social work and play, but from public health, the arts, developmental psychology, environmental sustainability and criminal justice. All agreed that incorporating a kindergarten stage into Scotland's universal state services had the potential to improve the long-term health, well-being and success of our society as a whole.

Back in 2015, the founding group had high hopes that the Early Level of Scotland's *Curriculum for Excellence* (which covers the care and education of three- to six-year-olds) could be adapted into a kindergarten stage fairly easily. Many politicians in Scotland admire the Nordic model so we hoped to attract public and cross-party political support for the notion of 'looking north' to their successful early years practice, rather than adopting the more schoolified approach currently infecting England and the USA.

Early childhood gets political

However, we soon recognised a potential barrier to success – the deeply-ingrained cultural acceptance, throughout Scotland and the rest of the UK, that instruction in the three Rs (reading, 'riting and 'rithmetic) should begin at the age of four or five, our traditional school starting age. The huge variation in developmental 'readiness' for literacy and numeracy among younger children means that most other countries around the world have a school start-date of six or seven. So our first task was to convince Scots that focusing throughout the Early Level on children's healthy all-round development (physical, emotional, social and cognitive) would not only further their future educational success but also contribute to their long-term health and well-being and a happier, healthier society.

Unfortunately, Upstart's inception coincided with political concern about a growing 'attainment gap' between children from high and low income households. In September 2015 the First Minister announced that, as part of a raft of measures to combat this gap, the government would introduce national standardised assessments in literacy and numeracy. And since her advisers were trapped in the old cultural paradigm about education, these would start in Primary 1, when children are four or five years old.

So, right from the beginning, those of us involved in Upstart found ourselves up to our necks in politics. Unsurprisingly, the SNP administration didn't welcome distractions from its attainment gap agenda so our attempts to interest them in a kindergarten stage fell on deaf ears. Then, in 2017, we organised an alliance of Scottish organisations to launch a 'Play Not Tests for P1' campaign to which all the opposition parties rallied, eventually leading to the passing of a vote in the Scottish

Parliament to scrap the tests. Since then, the SNP has suspected that Upstart is 'politically' motivated (which we are not).

Meanwhile, the Scottish government was also expanding state-funded ELC (early learning and childcare) to 1140 hours per year, practically doubling the entitlement for all three-year-olds and some two-year-olds, to begin in 2020. While in favour of this development (at least for three-year-old children), Upstart felt duty-bound to point out the problems the changes were causing on the ground – from ELC trainers with insufficient time and funds to prepare a high-quality workforce, to private nurseries for whom funding arrangements were causing enormous difficulties – all of which affected the welfare of children.

And when one of our supporters set up the Give Them Time (GTT) campaign for the right of parents to defer the school starting date for any four-year-old child (not just those born in January and February), we naturally added our voice to GTT's protests. One way and another, we therefore frequently found ourselves criticising local authority and government policy ... and thus living up to our name.

And now the good news. . .
On the other hand, there was plenty going on in Scotland for Upstart to applaud during the campaign's first five years. The launch of Scotland's Play Strategy in 2013 had brought the decline of play into the public arena and Inspiring Scotland funded several excellent projects to develop outdoor play. The Care Inspectorate made huge improvements to the overall quality of preschool education, especially in terms of getting young children outdoors, active and creative, and in promoting

the benefits of risk. There was a huge increase in outdoor provision in nursery settings and visits to 'forest school', while many full-time (private) outdoor nurseries were established around the country. And – partly due to support through Upstart meetings and social media activity – more and more P1 and P2 teachers began introducing play-based pedagogy in their classrooms.

Alongside this welcome emphasis on play, in 2017 another grassroots movement – ACE-Aware Nation – began drawing attention to the impact of 'adverse childhood experiences' on children's long-term health and the huge importance of supportive relationships with caring adults for their healthy development and well-being. Many key figures in the ACE-Aware Nation movement are also Upstart supporters so there have been many opportunities to learn from each other. Upstart, for instance, now defines our aim as 'a relationship-centred, play-based kindergarten stage'.

Over the last couple of years there have also been moves to incorporate the United Nations Convention on the Rights of the Child (UNCRC) into Scots law. At present, it's hoped this can be achieved by 2021. Again, Upstart has many supporters among children's rights activists and we are keen to offer our support. A high-quality kindergarten stage is clearly 'rights-focused' and there are many UNCRC Articles that support our aim, as well as UNCRC General Comment 7 on Early Childhood Care and Education (birth to eight years).

Realising the Ambition
On the whole, the education establishment was slow to accept the significance of play-based pedagogy for the under-sevens,

perhaps because of its own involvement in introducing the P1 literacy and numeracy assessments. We were therefore delighted in February 2020, when Education Scotland produced new practice guidance for early years settings – *Realising the Ambition: Being Me (RtA)*. It is a splendid document, taking a genuinely developmental approach and recommending play-based pedagogy across the Early Level, with plenty of emphasis on outdoor play and learning. If it had been published five years earlier, it's probable that the first Upstart meeting in Edinburgh wouldn't have happened and the idea of a kindergarten stage would never have been floated.

However, we've learned a lot during our first five years of campaigning, not least that those cultural assumptions about an early start on the three Rs run very deep. We're also aware that Scotland has a great many excellent policy documents which have not been successfully translated into practice. Rhetoric won't turn into reality without widespread understanding and support, not only from all the professionals involved but from the populace as a whole. Scotland needs a huge culture change in the way it views the care and education of the under-sevens.

For instance, the rapid expansion of funded pre-school provision is currently recommended, by politicians and media, as a way of (1) getting more parents into work and (2) improving children's educational outcomes. Neither aim suggests deep understanding of the developmental approach in *Realising the Ambition* (in which supporting young children simply to *Be Me* is of primary importance).

There are also currently no plans to scrap standardised national assessment of literacy and numeracy skills in Primary 1 and we regularly hear stories about local authorities pressurising schools for improved results, schools teaching to the tests and aspirational parents coaching their children to ensure they aren't 'left behind'. And there's a long way to go in ensuring regular access to outdoor play for all under-sevens, especially in natural environments. While many nursery settings have excellent provision, many do not. And when children transfer to school at four or five, it usually stops altogether.

Indeed, as long as the Early Level is split between nursery and school – in different buildings, with different staff qualifications, assessment and inspection regimes, adult-child ratios, etc. – it will be very difficult to fully realise Scotland's ambitions for early childhood.

Play is the Way

We hope that, by spreading the word about *Realising the Ambition* and its significance beyond the early years/primary sector, *Play is the Way* will help break down some of these barriers. We've divided the book into three sections:

- the case for relationship-centred, play-based learning up to the age of seven, argued from a variety of perspectives

- important factors for consideration in moving towards a developmentally appropriate 'kindergarten stage'

- the significance of early childhood care and education in terms of public health and social justice – this section has particular relevance for Scotland's intractable problem of the 'poverty-related attainment gap'.

Play is the Way was written during the summer of 2020, in a world struggling to control the spread of COVID-19, but our authors have tried to look beyond the COVID crisis. There is no way of knowing how or when it will end and – with nurseries and schools preoccupied with infection control – it's possible that practical responses to *Realising the Ambition* may be slightly delayed. On the other hand, the response to *RtA* has been so enthusiastic, and there's been so much related activity on social media during lockdown, it's just as possible that the response will be accelerated. There's certainly no doubt that relationship-centred, play-based pedagogy is the most appropriate educational approach for children traumatised by the five-month absence from school.

As I was writing this Foreword, news came through that the latest Good Childhood Report found UK children to be the 'most stressed' of all European children, often citing 'fear of failure' as the reason behind their anxiety. To anyone who understands child development, it's obvious that developmentally-inappropriate educational experiences before the age of seven have contributed to this mindset, just as they have been contributing to so many personal and social ills in UK society for 150 years.

We therefore hope this book will help early years practitioners and teachers to take the principles of *Realising the Ambition* forward in the coming years. But we also hope it will help policy-makers, community leaders and interested members of the public see the many benefits of a genuinely play-based Early Level and the damage caused to the next generation by expecting 'too much too soon' of children under seven years old.

SECTION ONE

What we know about where we want to go

Upstart supporters from a range of professional backgrounds consider the current state of play in early years (three to seven):

■ Dr Suzanne Zeedyk – a developmental neuroscientist – reflects on how Scotland's cultural history affects public attitudes to 'play-based' learning and explains why supportive relationships are an essential element of this approach to care and education.

■ The Chief Executive of Play Scotland, Marguerite Hunter Blair, surveys the evidence in favour of a kindergarten stage from a playwork perspective, describes Scotland's current policy position on play and considers the challenges of turning documentary rhetoric into real-life practice.

■ Dr Pam Jarvis – whose background is in education, history and psychology – takes issue with the 'myth of early acceleration' which has led to the 'schoolification' of early childhood care and education in the UK.

■ As Scotland prepares to incorporate the United Nations Convention on the Rights of the Child into Scots law, Cathy McCulloch (co-founder and co-director of the Children's Parliament) argues the Upstart case in terms of young children's rights.

■ Early years adviser Dr Elizabeth Henderson movingly describes how sensitive practitioners in a rights-focused, relationship-centred, play-based kindergarten stage can help Scottish education become more inclusive and equitable in the coming years.

Chapter 1
Relationships, play and learning in Scottish identity

Dr Suzanne Zeedyk

THE INTRODUCTION to this book tells how Upstart set out to change the structure of a system. . . and discovered that it really needed to change the mindset of a nation:

> In 2015, we had high hopes that [we could achieve] a kindergarten stage fairly easily. . . However, we soon recognised there was a potential barrier – the deeply ingrained cultural acceptance in Scotland that instruction in the three Rs should begin at the age of four or five.

That's an interesting challenge: to tackle a country's unconscious ideas about what their children need. It takes you into the misted realms of national and personal histories. In this chapter, I want to explore those histories, in order to shine light on why Upstart's campaign is sometimes greeted with discomfort.

Why should a vision based on straightforward child development principles be experienced as a threat? The more the sources of resistance are understood, the easier it is to see where opportunities for change lie. But there are also plenty of encouraging shifts underway in Scotland's wider societal landscape and I wish to reflect on those, especially the ones relating to 'relationships' and 'play', the two key elements in Upstart's vision of a kindergarten stage. By the end, I'll even be musing on the power of laughter.

'Learning' as a cultural value

Learning is a cultural value for Scotland. I don't think it too strong to claim that valuing academic learning is core to our national self-identity. Our esteem for the three Rs of reading, 'riting and 'rithmetic goes back a long way, at least to the seventeenth century. The Calvinist church believed it important to give all people direct access to the Bible and thereby to God. So they taught their boys **and** their girls to read. Author Daniel Defoe, writing in the eighteenth century, was so impressed by this that he remarked that England was 'a land full of ignorance', while in Scotland 'the poorest people have their children taught and instructed.'[1]

It's equally notable that Defoe's quote has been picked up and retained in contemporary use. Historian William Knox (2000) quotes it;[2] tour blogs quote it;[3] even the *Daily Mail* has quoted it.[4] The website 'Scotland Is Now', which exists to attract tourists, foreign students and immigrants to Scotland, proclaims this history proudly:

> Scotland has led the world in a commitment to excellence in education for centuries. We were the first country in the world to provide universal education open to both boys and girls, as early as the seventeenth century.[5]

This emphasis on universal academic learning has become part of the story Scotland tells itself and others of 'who it is'. (It is interesting to note that some historians suggest this acclaimed universal excellence is more myth than reality, but examining this will have to wait for another day. [6])

Moreover, it isn't only the academic learning we value, but also its start early in a child's life. Upstart has repeatedly made the point that our school starting age (the year children turn five) is premature and damaging in comparison to most other Western nations, where formal education starts at six or even seven. But when the Education (Scotland) Act of 1872 made education compulsory for children, it adopted the practice of existing Scottish church-led schools,[7] where the entry age was five. Since this was also the norm for other education systems within the British Empire, what alternative thinking could there possibly have been? It has left us, as Upstart puts it, 'trapped by history and tradition'.[8] I think, though, that our early starting age is not merely unconscious history. I think it is one that we are **proud of**.

I make this observation about self-identity because I personally believe it to be one of the main reasons Upstart has found it difficult to make the rapid headway predicted for establishing a kindergarten stage. The vision for play-based learning up to the age of seven years challenges more than Scotland's educational structure. It challenges Scotland's sense of itself. When you are proud of your cultural heritage of offering universal academic learning from an early age, how can you see yourself reflected in the converse image: play-based with a delayed 'start'?

Our continuing devotion to this academic heritage can be discerned in a range of nuanced ways.

■ *Newspaper photographs*. Newspapers reporting educational stories about young children seem inevitably to illustrate them with an 'academic' image. For example, two articles appeared whilst I was writing this chapter:

> On 27 July 2020, the *Herald Scotland* published a
> piece about trauma-informed approaches to
> teaching.[9] The accompanying photograph showed a
> teacher and child on the floor, talking, relaxed – and
> surrounded by shelves of books. The presence of the
> books signalled that this was a valid educational story.

> On 10 August 2020, the *Glasgow Evening Times*
> published a story about the funding of private
> nurseries.[10] What were the two three-year-olds in the
> associated image doing? Practising writing and pencil-
> holding.

■ *The phrase 'learning through play'*. It is true that our education system and wider culture are bringing play into focus (see Chapter Two). Yet we still seem anxious about the idea of children playing for the sake of playing. The phrase I hear used most often in schools, early years settings and policy documents is not 'play', but rather, 'learning through play'. Perhaps our culture needs reassurance that play has a purposeful value? Maybe we've achieved a shift towards play-based learning in early years precisely because the chosen terminology signals that play is virtuous? Clearly children aren't spending their time frivolously if they are **learning** through play.

■ *The PlayTalkRead Bus*. *PlayTalkRead* is a programme funded by the Scottish government. Its buses, painted a bright purple, travel round the country as venues for telling stories, sharing rhymes and having a good time in messy play. Since 2011, the buses have made it possible for countless young parents living in all sorts of communities to learn more about supporting their children's development. But would the campaign have been so successful if they had been called *PlayPlayPlay* Buses?

Somehow, the term 'playing' does not itself sound serious enough to the Scottish ear. That title would be unlikely to warrant funding through taxpayer contributions. The legitimacy of the buses is established through use of the word 'Read'.

How far back does Scotland's anxiety about play go? Probably to the very same period that established early, universal academic education. That Calvinist ethos was opposed to frivolity, on the grounds that fun did not offer a suitable path to God. In fact, it was dangerous. Play led you straight into the arms of the Devil himself.

Many older Scots remember swing parks being locked on a Sunday to stop children playing or enjoying themselves on the Sabbath. A 2016 *Guardian* article by Joan McFadden reminds us of the sorts of ordinary activities the Presbyterian Free Church regarded as frivolous:

> My dad was a minister in the Free Church. . . The
> range of potential sins meant we were banned from
> dancing, cinema, music, Guides, Scouts, sport and
> youth clubs. . . When my dad was given an old piano,
> he happily took lessons to play hymns but was
> ordered to get rid of the piano as a 'frivolous'
> instrument.[11]

Let's now think for a moment about the other component of Upstart's vision of a 'relationship-centred, play-based kindergarten stage'. Relationships were not part of the traditional philosophy for schooling. In part, this was due to class sizes. In state schools after the Education Act of 1872, primary classes could be as large as seventy pupils, especially in poorer areas. In Catholic schools, it could be double that, with 150 pupils for every one teacher.[12] Unsurprisingly, this yielded problems in maintaining discipline, leading to use of the leather tawse.

Classrooms were cold, learning methods were focused on repetition, and schools expected 'sustained quietness and instantaneous obedience'[13] None of this promoted any expectation of self-expression from children or warm relationships with teachers.

Recalling origins such as these helps put in context the many improvements that have been achieved within contemporary education. That ensures we do not take them for granted, and it also helps in thinking about how Upstart can best frame its goals for further change.

Relationships as a modern cultural value

Relationships are now flourishing across Scotland's schools. That shift in recent years has come through at least two overlapping routes: an emphasis on nurture and a better understanding of the biological impact of childhood trauma.

Nurturing approaches – which emphasise the importance of relationships in helping children to regulate emotions and behaviours – have been discussed for fifty years in UK school settings,[14] but have picked up particular intensity in Scotland over the past decade. After publication in 2013 of the Scottish government's policy document 'Better Relationships, Better Learning and Better Behaviour', nurture approaches were linked to solving challenges including the attainment gap, special educational needs and crime reduction. In 2013, the Education Department within the city of Glasgow initiated a nurture approach across all schools, entitled 'Towards a Nurturing City'.[15]

As the decade progressed, that emphasis on relationships

intensified. It was assisted by the unanticipated events of summer 2017, which saw screenings of the documentary film *Resilience: The biology of stress and the science of hope*[16] in communities across the country, led not by governmental bodies but by small grassroots organisations. The film explores discoveries made in the study of Adverse Childhood Experiences (ACEs) over the past two decades. Although various speakers, including myself, had been describing the science of ACEs to Scottish audiences for at least a decade, it was only through the medium of this film that public interest really took hold.

By the end of that summer a groundswell was under way, followed in 2018 and 2019 by major conferences under the banner of an 'ACE-Aware Nation', with two thousand or more people coming together to learn about the impact of childhood trauma. ACEs Hubs were set up by community members out of a spontaneous desire that others in their neighbourhood should share in this knowledge. This grassroots effort supplemented activity at governmental level, where the policy implications of ACEs knowledge were already under consideration. It is not too strong to say that Scotland now finds itself in the midst of an ACEs Movement, sharpened by critical debate, which is inspiring other regions of the world to embark on their own national conversations.

It must be emphasised that at the centre of the Scottish movement is a focus on relationships. A key insight from the ACEs research (and from work within related frames such as 'attachment' or 'trauma') is that stable, warm relationships are protective factors against trauma. Some critics of the ACEs framework have worried that this focus will be subsumed by attention to methods of scoring and measuring trauma. In Scotland, I believe we have succeeded in keeping relationships at the forefront of our thinking. In the large number of schools that have adopted a trauma-informed approach, closer attention is now given to the way staff respond to pupils and the way they make sense of behaviour. Relationship policies and nurture rooms are replacing the shame of behaviour policies and reward schemas. It does feel like a cultural shift is underway. Once you know about trauma, you can't unknow it.

Is it too early to say that a relational approach has become a modern cultural value for Scotland? Probably. A decade is not long, especially compared to the three centuries I reflected on earlier. There are many policy areas yet to tackle. However, there are also very encouraging developments underway that suggest we might just be on our way to a sustained cultural shift.

■ In 2018, Carol Craig called for Scotland to recognise the impact of its history as a 'belt happy culture,'[17] when hitting children with implements designed to cause pain was regarded as an ordinary way of dealing with behaviour, in both schools and homes. The flood of responses she received made clear how many people recognise and acknowledge they suffered negative long-term consequences of such treatment.

■ In 2019, the Scottish Parliament passed the Equal Protection from Assault Act, which gives children the same protection from assault that adults receive. The Act makes it illegal for children in Scotland to be hit by anyone – including their parents. Scotland joins sixty other nations in making this declaration about the kind of society we wish to be.[18]

■ In 2019, the Scottish government announced its plans to incorporate the United Nations Convention on the Rights of the Child (UNCRC) into domestic

Scots law. Scotland (along with the rest of the UK) became a signatory to this human rights treaty in 1999, but it has taken another 20 years to ensure that children's rights will be enforceable in the courts.[19]

■ In 2020, the Independent Care Review announced the outcomes of its three-year review of the quality of the care system. It made for uncomfortable reading: 'The review is damning in its condemnation of the current system and extensive in its recommendations for the future of care.'[20] Within hours of publication, though, the First Minister announced her intention to implement the recommendations, commenting that it was 'one of the most important moments in her tenure so far.'

■ In 2020, Education Scotland released new practice guidance for the early years workforce. The document, *Realising the Ambition: Being Me,*[21] has been warmly welcomed not only by the early years sector, but also by public health, children's rights, social justice and the arts, in part because it highlights young children's attachment needs and the importance of stable relationships in meeting those needs.

The final item in that list – the early years practice guidance – holds particular relevance for Upstart. As its chairperson, Sue Palmer, has stated publicly, 'I couldn't be more impressed with *Realising the Ambition.* The pedagogical approach it describes is exactly in line with the research on which we based our campaign.'[21] Attachment theory illuminates the theoretical rigour in Upstart's decision to advocate for a 'relationship-centred, play-based' pedagogy.

Attachment Theory:
Weaving together relationships, play and learning

The science of attachment explains why relationships play such a crucial role in children's development and why the presence of a safe adult has a physiological, calming effect on a child's behaviour. Dr John Bowlby, psychiatrist and paediatrician, is credited with its founding in the 1960s, which was followed by an explosion of scientific investigation lasting until this day. Attachment theory argues that children need relational experiences of both dependence and independence. Emotionally healthy development cannot occur without both. It is in understanding the intersection of those two categories of experience that the relevance of attachment for Upstart's aims becomes clear. Dependence and independence can be recast as 'relationships and play.'

John Bowlby is credited with the statement that 'Life is best organised as a series of daring ventures from a secure base'. It is an impressive achievement: the central message of attachment theory, summarised in a single, poetic sentence. In order for children to take risks in life – even ordinary growth risks like tackling new maths problems or resolving conflicts with friends or moving to a new school or eventually falling in love – they need to know there is a safe haven available in case things go wrong. Resilience requires experiences of **both** safety **and** threat. We can only grow by facing risks.

For children, supportive relationships are a fundamental form of safe haven. And play is a fundamental form of risk. Upstart's vision of a kindergarten stage fulfils Bowlby's mantra. In seeking a 'relationship-centred, play-based' experience, Upstart is calling on our education system to offer children daring ventures from a secure base.

One of the best ways to fully grasp the implications of Bowlby's sentence is through a simple schematic drawing of the *Circle of Security*. This is a conceptual model of the attachment process, developed in 1985 by three psychotherapists to support a parenting programme of the same name. Both the model and the programme deserve to be much more widely known.[23]

The model features three components:

    1) a 'safe haven' of waiting hands (safe base)

    2) 'supporting my exploration' (daring ventures, independence, play)

    3) 'welcoming me back' (safe base, dependence, familiarity).

Healthy development involves going around this cycle countless times every day. This applies to all human beings, whatever their age. For young children, the cycle is easier to see, for it is often performed as a literal, physical cycle, as when children run up a hill and then back again. At other times and for older children and adults, the cycle is a cognitive or emotional one, with internal risks and growth that cannot be so easily perceived.

The advantage of this model is that it illuminates the constant relationality of children's actions. Relationships are not the opposite of play. Healthy relationships do not reside in merely a safe base. Instead, in secure attachment, the sense of connection between adult and child is constant and reliable. That sense is present whether the child is resting in their safe haven or off on another daring venture. Relationships span **both** dependence **and** independence. Attachment theory argues that trust is the thread keeping adult and child emotionally connected, however far apart they are physically. The *Circle of Security* model graphically traces that pattern.

Once you realise the significance of the pattern, it becomes easy to spot in action. Parents who take part in the *Circle of Security* Parenting Programme articulate their insight powerfully:

> It wasn't anything I had ever heard of. It was something totally different that just clicked in my mind, with seeing how the kids go around the circle. . . The circle helps me have a picture of what's happening, all the time. . . You know why they are going out or coming in. And you can support them in both directions.[24]

Similar sentiments can be heard in professional networks of early years staff. For example, the team at Lullaby Lane Nursery, Bearsden have been developing skills in 'attachment-led practice':

> Now I have a whole new interpretation when I watch the children running up the hill or crawling in the tent or finally heading for the play kitchen after they've been comforted following morning drop off. Understanding the Circle of Security has given me a deeper understanding of what my role really is.

Unfortunately, most adults are never helped to see the pattern, so they understandably fail to appreciate its significance. Some may grasp it intuitively, but others end up misinterpreting children's actions, leaving them less able to meet a child's needs. Children need to trust the adults in their lives if they are to have the confidence of engaging in the daring educational ventures of play and learning.

One way to support Upstart's aim of a relationship-centred, play-based pedagogy would be to disseminate greater awareness of the *Circle of Security* model. By highlighting the integrated nature of relationships, play and learning, it helps grown-ups understand that these are not three separate domains of child development – they are interwoven.

Hopes for the future

It is an exciting time to be living in Scotland. There are many challenges, but also ground-breaking shifts underway in our beliefs about how children should be treated. The more robustly Upstart links its stated aims to this wider landscape, the greater the likelihood of achieving its hoped-for kindergarten stage.

Let me put that another way. The Introduction to this book tells how Upstart's founders came to see 'deeply ingrained cultural [beliefs]' about the nature of learning as a 'potential barrier' to restructuring the current educational system. But what if culture isn't the barrier? **What if culture is the point?** Perhaps Upstart's potential is not just in securing educational change but in helping to shift Scotland's sense of itself?

John Carnochan, one of the earliest voices to introduce the concept of Adverse Childhood Experiences to Scotland in his role as co-founder of the Violence Reduction Unit, was a keynote speaker at Upstart's 2018 AGM. His comments resonate with those I've made in this chapter.

> There's something about us, about our Calvinist genes. Why is it we don't like to be enjoying ourselves? Kids laughing and playing football. . . We don't like the idea, because they're a bit noisy. We don't enjoy the laughter.[25]

What if, in bringing more play to Scotland's education system, Upstart also brings more laughter to children's lives? That's what will happen when there is more play. There will be more giggling. It is inevitable. Schools will be noisier places. That counts as a profound vision. □

Chapter 2
'Play is a very misused adult word'

Marguerite Hunter Blair

> PLAY is a very misused adult word. To a child it is a way
> of life. To an adult it often means the unimportant
> recreational things we do when we are not working.
> Because this is the way we think of it for ourselves, we
> often dismiss it in children with the remark: 'Oh, he's
> just playing.' But the variety and function of play in a
> child's life is worthy of much more serious attention than
> this remark implies.
>
> Jean-Jacques Rousseau, Franco-Swiss Philosopher,
> 1762[1]

Why play matters

Play is an essential part of every child's life. It doesn't just
contribute to children's enjoyment of childhood – it's also
essential to their development. 'Just playing' is the key to healthy
growth and holistic development.

The importance of play in children's daily lives and healthy
development has become increasingly accepted in recent years.
An ever-growing body of evidence shows how this innate
behaviour contributes to children's quality of life, cognitive
development and executive function. However, there is still
much to be done to ensure children can play and thrive in the
early years – the most important sensitive period of their brain
development (defined by the United Nations as 0-8 years[2]).

Playworkers like myself know that play is crucial to achieving children's optimal health and well-being, whether it takes place indoors or outdoors, with or without adults, in spaces and places chosen by children and young people. We know that it is a powerful builder of happy, healthy, capable children, and that enjoying a wide range of play experiences in varied and stimulating settings helps foster resilience, creativity, curiosity, social skills and well-being. It also helps them learn about themselves and make sense of the environments around them. And self-directed play – when children have control over their choices of play experiences – doesn't just help children to thrive. It also, crucially, helps them learn how to learn. As Lester and Russell state in their Play England report:

> The act of playing has an impact on the architecture and organisation of the brain, and this leads to the emergence of more complex play forms, which in turn enables the establishment of an increasing repertoire of behavioural structures and strategies.[3]

It is not surprising then that play and child development are often seen as synonymous, particularly in the early years. Children need to have fun, creative, fulfilling and development-rich play experiences. The benefits of play in children's development can be summarised in the acronym SPICE: social, physical, intellectual, creative/cultural and emotional. As child development expert Susan Isaacs put it, 'play is the child's means of living and of understanding life.'[4]

Parents, early years providers and teachers therefore need to create play environments and offer materials that make play possible, providing stimulation linked to:

- social development – making and playing with

friends, learning how to share and relate informally with adults

■ physical development – playing on structures, fixed play equipment, natural features of the setting, playing games and engaging in spontaneous activities

■ intellectual development – problem solving, e.g. through den building and language games

■ creative/cultural development – pretend play, making things, paintings, go-karts, celebrating cultural events and festivals

■ emotional development of the self and others – through playing together, sharing, experiencing risk, frustration and a full range of feelings.

Two hundred years and we're still defending kindergarten!

In the words of Sturrock *et al,* 'Play stands at the centre of human development, especially in the formative years, but its import-ance has to be defended by each generation anew, often on different grounds.' [5]

The Upstart campaign for a kindergarten stage in Scotland has clearly articulated the importance of play in the early years for children to actively and interactively learn, become self-aware and acquire social rules. Play-based pedagogy has a far less formal approach to literacy and numeracy, and is centred around active (preferably outdoor) play. This makes it something all young children can engage with easily.

It's nearly two hundred years since the first kindergarten was started by Friedrich Froebel in Germany in 1837 (he was also the first to use the term 'playground' to describe play environments developed by adults for children). For Froebel, play and the outdoor garden, space and light, were fundamental to child development between the ages of three and seven.

Other early childhood pioneers such as Maria Montessori built on Froebel's work. Montessori (who famously said that 'play is the work of the child') believed the adult's role is to construct the environment in which children will learn best for themselves. She maintained that the essential dimensions of play are that it is voluntary, enjoyable, purposeful and spontaneous – and that interacting with their environments freely and with choice leads children to achieve their optimal development. Similarly, Loris Malaguzzi, founder of the Reggio Emilia approach to early years, believed in the power of the environment for children to thrive. His philosophy was that children are capable, collaborative and constructive learners, supported by a third teacher – the environment: 'There are three teachers of children: adults, other children and their physical environment.'[6]

Play was also fundamental to the theories of the two great developmental psychologists of the twentieth century – Jean Piaget and Lev Vygotsky. Piaget viewed play as integral to the development of intelligence in children. His theory argues that, as children mature, their environment and play should encourage further cognitive and language development. Vygotsky maintained that play makes two crucial contributions to children's developing abilities:

■ language and other human forms of 'symbolic representation'

■ the ability to control their own cognitive and emotional processes, or to 'self-regulate'.

These two abilities, language and self-regulation, are intimately inter-related[7] and together form some of the most powerful predictors of children's academic achievement and their emotional well-being[8].

In recent years, neuroscientific research has confirmed the findings of these early childhood pioneers and developmental psychologists but – as Suzanne Zeedyk points out in Chapter 1 – there still remains a feeling in Scotland that play is somehow 'frivolous'. So here we are, in 2020, still arguing the case for a kindergarten approach to the care and education of the under-sevens.

The contribution of the play sector

The work of the play sector is more wide-ranging than that of Upstart, being concerned with the importance of play across the lifespan. The sector has commissioned a number of policy-oriented literature reviews on play for children and young people, including *Play for a Change* (2008)[9], *Getting it Right for Play: Power of Play* (2012)[10] and *The Play Return: A review of the wider impacts of play initiatives* (2014).[11] These reviews and evaluation reports have concluded that playing leads to a wide range of interconnected beneficial outcomes for children, including:

■ cognitive development (e.g. language skills, problem solving and independent learning skills, self-efficacy, gaining perspective, representational skills, memory and creativity)

■ physical health and development (e.g. physiological, cardiovascular and fine and gross motor skills development as well as increased physical activity)

- mental health, happiness and emotional well-being (e.g. building confidence, improved child/parent attachments, coping with stress, tackling anxieties and phobias, aiding recovery in therapeutic contexts, and alleviating the symptoms of ADHD for some children)

- social development (e.g. working with others, sharing, negotiating and appreciating others' points of view)

- risk management and resilience through experiencing and responding to unexpected, challenging situations.

Tim Gill, an advocate of adventurous play, concluded that 'from the perspective of politicians and policy makers. . . investing in play can, and does, lead to multiple benefits including improved educational attainment, a healthier society and increased levels of tolerance within and between communities.'[11]

In 2013 Play Scotland supported the Scottish government in producing a Play Strategy[12], setting out the value of play as a life-enhancing daily experience for all our children in their homes, nurseries, early childcare settings, schools and communities. It recognised every child's right to play and to participate in play activities and experiences, in line with Article 31 of the United Nations Convention on the Rights of the Child (UNCRC).[13]

This right was established in 1989, when the UNCRC was first published, and in 2013 the UN Committee on the Rights of the Child provided further guidance to support children's playing and learning. It states that the rights described in Article 31 'contribute to all aspects of learning' and education must be directed to the 'development of the child's personality, talents and mental and physical abilities to the fullest potential.'[14]

The 'right to play' is fully examined in UNCRC General Comment 17 (2013),[15] linking Article 31 rights to health, well-being, creativity, imagination, self-confidence, self-efficacy, participation and inclusion. The Committee recognises play as 'a fundamental and vital dimension of the pleasure of childhood, as well as an essential component of physical, social, cognitive, emotional and spiritual development' and states that:

> inclusive education and inclusive play are mutually
> reinforcing and should be facilitated during the
> course of every day throughout early childhood
> education and care (preschool) as well as primary
> and secondary school. While relevant and necessary
> for children of all ages, play is particularly significant
> in the early years of schooling.[16]

As Bob Hughes confirms in *A Playworker's Taxonomy of Play Types*,[17] a balanced diet of play is the obvious key to unlocking a wide range of necessary learning, development and health benefits. This is echoed by developmental psychologist David Whitebread:

> Play in all its rich variety is one of the highest
> achievements of the human species, alongside
> language, culture and technology. Indeed, without
> play, none of these other achievements would be
> possible. Psychological research has established that
> there are five fundamental types of human play. These
> are commonly referred to as: physical play, play with
> objects, symbolic play, pretence or socio-dramatic
> play, and games with rules. Each supports a range of
> cognitive and emotional developments, and a good
> balance of play experience is regarded as a healthy
> play diet for children.[18]

As our understanding of play types continues to evolve, the

challenge is to ensure that the practices necessary to facilitate them are adopted in early years. If we take a moment to listen to children playing we can hear joy and fun. If we watch children playing we can see that it is something that comes naturally to them. It is an intrinsic part of who we all are as humans. We can all be playful even as adults but, if we do not allow young children the space, time, permission and freedom to play, that playfulness may not fully develop.

The state of play in present-day Scotland

Since publication of the Early Years Framework (2008),[19] which committed to 'improving outcomes and children's quality of life through play', Scotland has developed a strong policy framework that supports children's right and need to play and its Play Strategy is underpinned by principles of inclusion and sufficiency, affirming that:

> Play encompasses children's behaviour which is freely chosen, personally directed and intrinsically motivated. It is performed for no external goal or reward and is a fundamental and integral part of healthy development – not only for individual children but also for the society in which they live.[20]

The Play Strategy also acknowledges that play contributes to flagship public policies in Scotland such as improving attainment, health and reducing inequality.

The Planning (Scotland) Act 2019[21] goes a step further and legislates for children's play. It places a statutory duty on local authorities to undertake Play Sufficiency Assessments (PSAs) as part of their strategic planning and for children to be consulted on local place plans. This complements the Scottish government's commitment to incorporate the UNCRC into Scots law by 2021.

Playful learning indoors and outdoors is also a part of Scotland's *Curriculum for Excellence*, much-valued by early years practitioners, teachers and sector partners, as well as children. *Active Learning in the Early Years* (2007)[22], *Building the Ambition* (2014)[23] and *Realising the Ambition: Being Me* (2020)[24] all recognise the need for children to have a curriculum that ensures sufficient time for children to play uninterrupted. The last document is supported by the *Play Pedagogy Interactive Toolkit* for *Curriculum for Excellence* Early Level[25], which attempts to embed a consistent, qualitative approach to play pedagogy that will deliver the practices and benefits of a kindergarten stage.

Clearly, on paper, Scotland couldn't be in a better place. But – as everyone in public and third sector services knows – translating documentary rhetoric into real-life practice can be extremely challenging. There has always been, and arguably still is, a lack of understanding, consistency and quality in application of the above measures. This appears to be related to Scotland's cultural attachment to academicised educational approaches (see Chapter 1).

Over the last few decades, the restrictions on learning environments imposed through the traditional school model in Scotland have collided with curbs on children's out-of-school opportunities for free play (e.g. traffic-clogged streets, parental fears of 'stranger danger' and the ready availability of indoor sedentary entertainment). This has resulted in a sedentary and non-interactive lifestyle for very many young children. In 2017, the Gateshead Millennium Study[26] found that by the time children were aged seven, they spent half their day sitting, and by the age of 15 this has gone up to three-quarters of their day spent sitting. Activity levels tailed off from around the time of going to school – at four or five years of age – when lifestyle changes meant children were seemingly being 'trained' to be more sedentary and inactive.

Today's young children need the help of adults to provide opportunities for active, self-directed social play – and access to the outdoors – more than any previous generation. But, although playworkers and early years specialists are well aware of this, many other adults still don't recognise the value of play for children's learning and development, and the significance of a rich environment both indoors and out. The scale of this challenge cannot be underestimated.

The play sector can occupy a significant role in developing resources to support early years practitioners in developing effective practice to support children's learning through play. Play Strategy resources developed by the play sector like the *Loose Parts Play Toolkit*[27] have broadened the play opportunities and environments of children, and increased the confidence of adults working with children in a range of settings. Play Scotland has recently produced *Playful Pedagogy,*[28] a practical guide with resources and case studies designed to help introduce and support everyday learning adventures across the school. It makes play experiences central to learning, giving pupils the flexibility to find their own solutions to both new and existing problems. It engages children in personally meaningful activities, learning about themselves and others, and encourages autonomy and motivation.

Conclusion

It's clear that Scotland as a society is moving in the right direction in ensuring all children are afforded their right to play. However, there is still much work to be done before we can assume the importance of that right is fully embedded in the national consciousness. We still need challenge, change and improvement in schools to ensure that the ambition for Scotland's youngest children is realised. We also need co-learning between a range of professionals and practitioners such as playworkers, play therapists, occupational therapists and educationalists to share expertise with one another and inform effective practice and training on play pedagogy.

Upstart has two key roles to play in this undertaking: continuing to support playing and learning in the context of children's rights and child development; and providing a practical narrative on how to fully implement playful pedagogy across Scotland. □

Chapter 3
The myth of early acceleration

Dr Pam Jarvis

Defining the problem

In 1999 a short book in the *Darwinism Today* series included a paragraph that serves as a useful 'thought bubble' for early years education: 'Accept that there is such a thing as human nature and seek to find out more about it, so that policies can be grounded on the best available evidence of what human beings are like.'[1]

If we start from this premise in terms of educational policy, we need to begin with the model of childhood that has emerged from a century of empirical study in both psychology and neuro-biology. As pointed out by Harvard's Centre on the Developing Child, 'brains are built, over time, from the bottom up.'[2]

So how does this compare to contemporary teaching guru Doug Lemov's principle that teachers should: '. . . begin with the end. . . The only criterion that determines the success of an activity is. . . whether you achieved an objective that can be assessed.'[3]

Does teaching and learning really consist of creating fixed objectives and then attempting to transfer 'content' directly from adults' to children's minds?

This mismatch between what a human child actually 'is' and a 'top-down' pedagogical approach is especially problematic for teachers working with children of six or under, because – at this very early stage in their lives – they are engaged in building the foundations of understanding: they have a very limited pool of existing knowledge to draw upon to try to make sense of incoming information. It is thus impossible to 'begin at the end' with them because they're at such an early stage of building their cognitive architecture that there is little for the incoming constructs to hang upon.

It's like throwing a piece of clothing into a wardrobe with no suitable hangers – such 'transmissions' fall to the bottom and lie tangled together in the darkness. To continue the wardrobe analogy, when a new garment arrives that could be coordinated with existing items, it's difficult or impossible to find them in the tangle that lies at the bottom.

Building brains from the bottom up

Crone *et al* propose there are three major developmental cycles, from birth to three, three to six and six to ten.[4] This has a broad similarity with Piaget's stage theory in which a child builds mental structures called schemas from incoming information. These schemas progressively coordinate in a 'spreading activation' fashion.[5] This enables the child to engage in increasingly abstract thought as the network expands, building intricate interconnections between schemas. The result of this is an exponentially expanding ability to use previously learned knowledge to make sense of incoming information.

As children build their knowledge base, they become able to process larger amounts of information more quickly by flexibly 'chunking' ideas. For example, as childhood unfolds, cats will be linked both to a 'domestic pets' schema which will also include dogs and rabbits and then later to a 'feline animals' schema which will take in lions and tigers. As the child gains further in maturity and experience she will form yet more abstract connections, for example to the musical 'Cats'.

To continue the 'brain as wardrobe' analogy, the hangers slowly appear and the garments are coordinated into mix and match outfits in the wardrobe: incoming information now enters a network of connections. As this process unfolds, the child becomes increasingly able to follow adult agendas because they have many more routes in existing cognition through which they are able to 'connect'.

Whitebread and Basilio explain that the growing coordination of the developing cognitive architecture results in a gradual increase in the ability to focus attention, to be in control of one's own actions, to resist distraction and to engage in goal directed activity.[6]

'Working memory' – the cognitive mechanism by which human beings bring together previously learned knowledge and incoming information in order to achieve understanding – gradually matures within this burgeoning network of coordinated thought. However, all of this relies upon building from the bottom up. 'Inputting' from the top down resembles pouring water from a jug into a glass or putting a memory stick in a PC and starting a file transfer. And human brains simply cannot be built from such a process because this is not how human beings evolved; it is not what they are 'like'.

The developing brain

Susan McConnell from Stanford University creates a useful analogy for the initial 'wiring' process undertaken by the human brain. She comments:

> Think of the brain as a telephone exchange. It makes its first connections on very basic information. For example, when you start to create a national telephone network, you would first of all connect up all the major cities; one of the first projects might be laying one main telephone line from New York to Boston. Once that initial link is made, when you ring out to Boston from New York, all the phones in Boston will ring. As time goes by, you would gradually construct lines to all the different houses in Boston. Eventually, when you want to ring your grandmother in Boston, you can do so in the knowledge that only her phone will ring.[7]

Just as in the wardrobe analogy, we are looking at incoming information having something to attach to and moving from the general to the particular as more connections – or hangers – are added. And sometimes, this involves processes which may conversely seem more like forgetting than remembering. A good illustration of this is children's early language learning. In *Accents are Forever* Keister points out:

> 6-month-olds in Tokyo perceive the difference between l and r just as easily as babies in Seattle. But by the time the same infants are a year old, they have lost that ability. Instead, they zero in on the "home" sounds and tune out unfamiliar ones. The first language keeps fighting off the pronunciations of a new language.[8]

This relates to a process which is not just about the creation of neuronal connections, but the strengthening of some and the atrophy of others. This works rather like a 'housekeeping' process in which the cognitive architecture is constantly maintained for maximum efficiency.

When children first arrive in the world, they create huge numbers of neuronal pathways during their initial interactions with the physical and social world. But as time goes by, some of these pathways are pruned and others are strengthened on the basis of differential usage. In this way, the brain undergoes a continual adjustment programme directed by the flow of 'traffic' that ensues. Some pathways go on to become the equivalent of four-lane motorways, some become broad, well-maintained B roads and yet others fade to simple tracks. It is analogous to the way in which a large number of people walking across a wooded area will eventually create an increasingly obvious pathway.

Blooming and pruning

Brown and Jernigan summarise the current state of knowledge with respect to neuronal development in the early years:

> At age four. . . some regions of the cortex are notably decreasing in volume while others are strongly increasing. . . Consistent with the theme of dramatic architectural 'blossoming' in the brain within the preschool years, changes in cortical volume show an early period of striking, widespread expansion that eventually gives way to selective reductions across the cortex by around the ages of puberty.[9]

The creation and pruning of connections in the brain never really ceases. However, childhood is the life stage of major construction and throughout this period different areas of cognition 'bloom and prune' on different schedules.

Tierney and Nelson propose that in the case of visual and auditory perception, significant pruning occurs until sometime between the fourth and sixth year of life, whilst pruning in areas involving higher cognitive functions continues until the end of adolescence.[10] They comment that this process is essential for human beings because of their evolved capacity to attune and flexibly respond to the physical and social environment into which they are born.

A related process which goes on alongside is the myelination of the brain – the laying down of a fatty substance around neuronal connections that performs a similar function to insulating tape around electrical wiring, i.e. helping signals to transmit more effectively. Again, with respect to the higher cognitive functions, this process is not complete until the end of adolescence. Tierney and Nelson conclude: 'although basic sensation and perception systems are fully developed by the time children reach kindergarten age, other systems such as those involved in memory, decision making, and emotion continue to develop well into childhood.'[11]

How then can we expect to accelerate such an organism, when the 'wiring' of a young child's brain is at such an early stage of construction? The human developmental process evolved over millions of years, with its roots in pre-human species. This is the basis of what human beings 'are like' and attempts at acceleration will not change this. But acceleration may certainly have emergent *negative* results.

The emotion-cognition cascade

It is impossible to over-rev a car with an engine that is not yet fully built, and this is the issue that we have to contend with when we attempt to accelerate children, particularly in the first seven years. Children whom adults attempt to 'accelerate', whose 'cognitive engine' is being worked too hard at a stage when pieces of it are still not properly connected will inevitably feel stress as they struggle to cope.

The stress will be even greater if – due to age-related expectations and standardised assessments – they come to feel that they are a source of disappointment. And such experiences do not only have an effect upon the emotions, but also upon the cognitive process as stress hormones fill the body and brain. Hence attempts to accelerate children risk creating the opposite effect to the one that is intended – it can actually *damage* their readiness to learn.

Raymond *et al* explain:

> 'The main brain structures that are affected by the chronic secretion of stress hormones during childhood (hippocampus, prefrontal cortex and amygdala) are differentially involved in various cognitive functions (memory, emotion regulation, encoding of emotional memories, etc.).' [12]

Cortisol is the main stress hormone. Wagner *et al* linked higher cortisol levels to reduced function across three cognitive domains: inhibitory self-control, flexibility and emergent metacognition, which relates to monitoring one's own thinking processes. All these processes are essential to behaviours that underpin learning, such as focusing attention, concentration and problem solving. [13]

Given that we now know so much about how such processes develop during the long, slow human development period, why would we start children off in education from an entirely erroneous premise of mind-to-mind programming? And why would we further exacerbate this issue by adding the stress of unreasonable expectation and a high risk of failure? The answer is, presumably, because those who create such 'pedagogy' are not starting from the premise of what the human being actually *is*, but what they would prefer it to be.

Learning about 'Being Me'

The disparity of an 'acceleration curriculum' applied to young children can be compared to Buzz Lightyear's misunderstanding of the type of creature that he is, featured at the beginning of *Toy Story 1*. And just like Buzz, children need to move through a learning process about themselves in terms of how their biology works, and what this means with respect to what they can do and when.

The advantage children have over Buzz, of course, is that they are not manufactured toys but complex biological organisms that grow and develop. But they can only do this if given sufficient time and a nurturing programme that is fit for purpose. This is why *Realising the Ambition* – Scotland's new practice guidance for Early Level – is subtitled *Being Me*.[14]

Young children enter education with neuronal architectures that have been constructed in different family and community environments, and from slightly different genetic bases. Their existing knowledge will be uneven in terms of literacy and numeracy, and they will vary in their level of physical development.

This is particularly the case where a cohort of children have birthdays across an entire calendar year. A four-year-old has had 25 per cent less time in the world than a five-year-old, the same difference between an eight-year-old and a ten-year-old. Early Years teachers need to be sensitive to this, to meet each child 'where s/he is', providing the experiences, support and nurturance that is needed, rather than pushing them through 'instructional' procedures that take no account of their organic developmental processes.

Scotland's education pioneer Robert Owen (1771-1858) proposed 'judicious farmers will not prematurely put their beasts of burden to work.'[15] This is just as salient for children in the present as it was for the children in Owen's New Lanark school two hundred years ago.   □

Chapter 4
Children's rights and the move towards a kindergarten stage

Cathy McCulloch

THE VISION embedded in the United Nations Convention on the Rights of the Child (UNCRC) [1] is that children grow up in a world of love and understanding. A Bill to incorporate the UNCRC into Scots law was brought before the Scottish Parliament in Autumn 2020 and it is expected the Act will be brought into Scots law 'fully and directly' in Spring 2021.

So – we have a wonderful opportunity to bring in additional measures in Scotland that will help to keep children healthy, happy and safe. Who wouldn't support that? Well, lots of people actually.

What do children's rights mean?

When it comes to children's human rights, the tendency to equate 'having rights' with 'getting what you want' is arguably a peculiarly Scottish trait. For instance, a well-respected colleague described how, when he'd told his son to tidy his room before dinner, the response was 'I don't have to do what you tell me, my teacher says I have rights'. He followed this by challenging me, 'So, what do you say to that?'

It struck me forcibly that if this respected academic could think that in any world it would be okay for a six-year-old to tell his dad he wasn't going to tidy his room because he 'has rights' we're in more trouble than I thought.

The idea of 'getting what you want' may terrify adults – but I know from my work with Children's Parliament[2] that it terrifies children more.

Children's security is tied up with the feeling that the adults around them know what they're doing and are 'in control'. Children like having boundaries – different families have different boundaries but the important thing for children is that their boundaries are consistent. No child I've ever met really wants to be able to do whatever they want.

Working in the area of children's rights in Scotland is often a lonely and uncomfortable place to be. In conversations and meetings, I've watched people drift off, glaze over, indeed even fall asleep once or twice. Many people who do fantastic work with and for children have a real block when it comes to recognising the potential that embedding a children's human rights approach has in improving and even, transforming, children's lives. But with the incorporation of the UNCRC we will *all* be required not only to know what children's rights are, but also to make sure we're upholding them.

Children's rights in early years. . . and Scotland's culture

Children's early years are the perfect time to begin to develop habits of a lifetime. What better habits to develop than kindness, trust, empathy and respect for human dignity – none of which can be taught but all can be developed through relationships with adults who live these qualities every day, qualities that are the foundation of a human rights approach.

Scotland has a long-held commitment to the welfare of children, whether that be neighbours keeping an eye on each other's children or early years practitioners and teachers making sure food and clean clothes are available for children in need. But while this 'looking out for children' is important, it's just as important that children have opportunities to develop the skills and qualities they need to help keep them healthy, happy and safe throughout their lives.

The United Nations Committee on the Rights of the Child issues supplementary information on the UNCRC through General Comments. General Comment No7 relates to early childhood, which it defines as birth to eight. It states:

> A shift away from traditional beliefs that regard early childhood mainly as a period for the socialisation of the immature human being towards mature adult status is required. The Convention requires that children, including the very youngest children, be respected as persons in their own right. Young children should be recognised as active members of families, communities and societies, with their own concerns, interest and points of view.[3]

And Professor Laura Lundy, Queen's University Belfast, writes: 'Suggesting that a child's well-being is affected adversely is powerful in itself, but ostensibly not as powerful as arguing that their human rights have been breached.'[4]

Thinking about Scotland's 'traditional beliefs', I would argue that our current cultural norms impact significantly on our willingness and ability to embrace the children's human rights agenda.

The legacy of 'children should be seen and not heard' casts a long shadow. Children's place in society is determined by adults and the extent to which children are able to influence and inform our policy and practice so that it better reflects children's own lived experiences varies according to the particular adults whom children happen to have in their lives.

Whilst most people would agree we want children to grow up ready for 21st century life and work, we don't tend to start taking this seriously until children are well into their teens and have already developed ways of thinking and behaving based on their early childhood experiences. We teach compliance instead of encouraging curiosity, politeness instead of questioning and acceptance in place of challenge. Establishing curiosity, questioning and an ability to think critically in early childhood are essential principles for protective and critical thinking and a level of agency that will last through life.

Rewards and punishments

Picture the scene: children are in the middle of their 'free play' time, groups of children are taking part in various activities. Suddenly a fight breaks out between three of the children and toys are thrown, accidentally hitting another child. The adult in charge responds by stopping all the activities, tells off the children involved in the fight and says that because of their behaviour free play is over and everyone should go and sit on the carpet. It might not happen in your setting, but according to children, this practice is still commonplace.

Our prevailing culture sets an expectation that if a child does something wrong they should be punished. Why? What is it we're trying to achieve? Isn't it that the child learns to do better next time? And if we know – as we do – that this result is more likely to be achieved through kind and loving relationships where a child is supported to understand why they behaved in the way they did, and helped to think about what they could do better next time, then why not change our approach?

This is not to say there shouldn't be consequences for inappropriate behaviour, but how we respond to the behaviour is an opportunity rich in learning for a child. When children are trusted to try and work things out for themselves, they learn to negotiate, compromise, take risks, speak up for themselves and others. Article 3 of the UNCRC focuses on children's 'best interests'. Children's best interests are served by putting the needs of the child at the heart of our work, not adults' need to be 'in control'.

And – last word on culture: the really wonderful thing about embedding a human rights approach is that children gain power. They are empowered to speak up and know this is not just an option but an expectation. This too can often terrify adults.

Initiative-itis

As the needs and impact of childhood experiences become more visible through a growing body of evidence, and the issues seemingly ever more testing, there is an understandable tendency to reach for 'the next new thing' in an attempt to get to grips quickly with entrenched challenges. We have seen the emergence of initiatives supporting kindness, nurture, confidence, well-being and the recent prominent work around childhood trauma. The ACEs movement has effectively reached new audiences and has had a significant impact in helping raise people's understanding of the effect of childhood trauma across a person's life. Each of these initiatives offers information, new understanding, new activities. . . all undoubtedly useful.

However, what they don't offer is consistency in approach or sustainability.

If we take into account the prevailing cultural and traditional beliefs mentioned earlier, we can see that those strong influences and expectations largely dictate how we approach and deliver work with children. The way individual heads lead their establishment is left entirely to them and as long as a nod is given to current national policy they can pretty much lead with whatever focus they believe in most strongly.

This is why I have witnessed great practice at a local level being replaced by the ideas and motivations of a new establishment head. In a setting which had focused heavily on nurture with all the information packs, toolkits and other resources that were provided to support the work, staff now found the new head wanted to replace the nurture agenda with 'kindness' and so – rather like a children's football team where all eleven players charge after the ball at once with no thought to positioning – staff had to drop all the nurture resources and transfer their interest and allegiance to 'kindness'.

Of course there is a lot of common ground across all the initiatives that will be familiar, but unless and until we have a consistent approach across all of children's lives, they will be at the mercy of whatever initiative or practice, wacky or wonderful, that individual heads feel is the one their own values most align with.

Instead of leaving the development of values and practice to individuals, imagine if we had a consistent and sustainable approach that required *all* of us to embrace and implement, an approach that encompasses every single initiative known to wo/man. Yep, you've guessed it – a human rights approach *requires* adults to be kind, loving, understanding, nurturing, and put respect at the heart of all our relationships.

In the early years (birth to eight) that approach would involve a system of education and care that is rights-focused, relationship-centred and play-based.

A quick word about participation

There are worrying signs that some people, and often in management roles, are equating participation with children's human rights. We see children being marched into a 'participation event' where adults fire questions at them, write up what children say and hey presto – bish, bash, bosh, job done.

Participation is an important element of a human rights approach, but can't be the whole story. You wouldn't expect to be invited to a local community planning event to share your views about your community and then, when someone threatens you as you walk home, be told by the police that 'you had your human rights at the participation event'.

Children's human rights are universal, inalienable, non-divisible and interdependent. They belong to everyone under 18, they can't be taken away by adults, we can't choose which rights we're 'giving' and which we're 'taking away' and they all depend on each other.

Prevention is better than cure

As Florence Nightingale said, 'There are many more hands ready to pick us up when we fall than there are to prevent us from falling in the first place.' This certainly still seems to be the case in the UK today.

While we adults spend our time fighting our individual corners and continuing to 'do' to and for children, too many children are neglected, unheard, abused and forgotten. We spend a great deal of time talking about the impact on children of poverty, disadvantage, poor parenting, chaotic families and more. Impossible amounts of money go to work that supports children and families in dealing with the impact of the trauma they experience.

On the other hand, a tiny percentage of time is spent thinking about how we can prevent trauma occurring in the first place. This is understandable, the challenges are great. However, if we know, as we do, that embedding human rights makes a difference in the way we build the environments around children and families, then we should put our individual agendas aside and come together to think through how we can support the emergence of a growing network of knowledgeable and committed individuals and organisations and #makerightsreal.

It's no coincidence that the Nordic countries, which currently lead the world in terms of childhood well-being (and which Upstart frequently cites as examples of good early years practice) take a UNCRC rights-based approach from the very start of children's lives.

Empowering children to think for themselves

A few years ago my colleagues and I were working in a nursery and primary school in Fife. The remit was to support the school to develop a 'whole school community approach to children's rights and participation'.

My team took life-size wooden cut outs of Happy Hannah,

Healthy Harry and Safe Sam which we used to help the children think about what Hannah, Harry and Sam need in their lives to help keep them safe, healthy and happy. The children said things like 'five pieces of fruit a day' and 'hold your mummy's hand when you cross the road' and also 'someone to love you, cuddles' and 'people to be nice to you'.

I then held up our 'Big Book of Promises' – a papier maché prop that contains the UNCRC. I told the children that the 'Big Book of Promises' is a list of promises adults have made to children to keep children safe, healthy and happy. I asked the children if they knew adults are not allowed to do whatever they want to children. The children replied that they didn't know this.

I explained that no adult is allowed to hurt children or make them feel scared or worried, even adults in your family or adults who are friends. I also explained that we know not all children are safe, healthy or happy but the most important thing is that you know that adults have made promises to look after children and if you ever feel worried or scared you must talk to an adult you trust. At that point a wee girl jumped up off the carpet, clenched her fists and shouted 'Oh WOW!' The nursery staff later told me she was three and a half years old.

Scotland's opportunity to get it right from the start

We all have a responsibility to ensure children have the knowledge that there are laws in place to protect them. Think about the times another child abuse scandal hits the headlines and how much time we spend talking about what happened, who are the abusers and what should happen to them. Shouldn't we be thinking about what needs to be in place to reduce the risk of possible harm in the first place? A human rights approach would ensure children had knowledge and were empowered to speak up. Adults would know children will speak up if they are harmed. It's out in the open – children are empowered, adults are informed. It's a good start.

A human rights approach helps to create the foundations for a strong and compassionate society, rooted in the shared values of kindness, trust, empathy and respect for human dignity. Opportunities to develop such qualities start at birth; qualities that can't be taught but rather grow out of lived experiences. We are all, individually and collectively, responsible for ensuring our children know they have human rights that will help to keep them safe, healthy and happy.

Children get this. Now we just need adults to catch them up. The incorporation of the UNCRC into Scots law gives us the opportunity to get it right from the start – and General Comment 7 is an excellent starting point. I advise all advocates for a kindergarten stage to read it and use its principles to help move the Upstart Scotland campaign forward. ☐

Chapter 5
See me, hear me, walk with me on my journey: inclusion, diversity and equity

Dr Elizabeth Henderson

Walk with me

Aidan didn't speak a word to me the whole time he was in nursery. But now and then he looked at me out of the corner of his eye, from a safe distance. I wanted to be in his world, to see things as he did, to better understand him. But I could only observe, over and over again, listen intently and try to feel and intuit my way there, learning that every gesture, sound or look carried deep meaning; he spoke a language I had to learn.

Across the nursery garden Malek sat alone with some sticks, finding it difficult to interact with the other children and adults, unable to reach out and to bond. He watched as Magda and Faith walked hand-in-hand across the nursery garden towards Aidan, who was now rocking back and forth by the fence and looking through the leaves of the rowan tree, as shafts of sunlight sparkled and danced. The girls, neither of whom spoke English as their first language, had quickly become best friends, and were dropping off apples, bread, butter and potatoes from their supermarket delivery van.

Each child, like a springtime fledgling, simply trying to find their way in the world; trying to write the beginning of their story, their life's narrative. Each child, in need of a special friend willing to reflect back to them their strengths and gifts, their potential life's narrative. Each child, in need of an understanding

63

practitioner – willing to listen, willing to wonder, willing to walk with them on their journey and help them build a strong life-narrative. Each child, wanting to belong. Each child, wanting to be known.

Who cares?

In 1937 Susan Isaacs, commenting on the value of nursery schools wrote: 'Above everything else, a child needs warm human relationships, and spontaneous feelings of friendliness.'[1] That has not changed; children today still need warmth, a sense of belonging and to feel included. But is this happening?

Inequality in our society is both historical and political. Yet, despite a plethora of government documents advocating for the inclusion and rights of all children, society remains divided and stratified. The current pandemic has highlighted these inequalities, revealing the gaps that exist between rhetoric, guidance, legislation and practice – be that in the NHS, the care sector or early learning and childcare. Following years of cutbacks, underfunding and under-resourcing as a consequence of the commodification of services, professionals working in these sectors find themselves struggling, in over-stretched contexts, to provide the necessary care for the elderly, the sick and the young. Inevitably, those most at risk and in need of our support are the most likely to be detrimentally affected.

In Scotland today, 30.9 per cent of school age children are recognised as having an additional support need.[2] The Education (Additional Support for Learning) (Scotland) Act 2004[3] and further guidance in 2017[4] introduced a series of additional support needs ranging from dyslexia, emotional and social difficulties and motor or sensory impairments to families experiencing substance misuse, bereavement, chronic illness and learning disabilities. These support needs fall broadly into four categories: learning environment, family circumstances, disability or health needs and social and emotional factors.[5]

Until 2004, for many people, the idea of additional support and the use of the term 'inclusion' related mainly to disability. This is an example of what Sara Ahmed calls the *stickiness* of language[6] – particular associations with a word embed themselves so deeply in our minds that hearing or seeing that word conjures up those particular notions, concepts, feelings and meanings. Words are therefore sticky with meaning.

It is possible, therefore, that inclusion for some might still be associated only with disability. However, in today's world inclusion has to go much further than the legislation in 2004 as research clearly shows that gaps in outcomes for many children are related to inequalities in society and exacerbated by poverty, race, gender, ethnicity, homelessness – to name a few.

Some children, however, are marginalised by the education and care sector itself because historically education in the UK over-privileges the value of thinking and cognition along with the ability to later regurgitate facts. This leads to a system that (un)intentionally marginalises those whose gifts and skills may be related to other ways of knowing and being. Children with a natural inclination towards art, music, sport, craft, and social and emotional intelligences are therefore undervalued and marginalised (un)intentionally. Just like those children who need more time to develop, learn and grow, they need and deserve our recognition and support. No child should be excluded or feel they do not belong just because 'they are different' – when, in fact, we are all different.

The prevailing system perpetuates the status quo for those in power – predominantly white, male, middle class and able bodied. So those in power remain in power and those on the edge remain under-valued, their evolving life's narrative punctuated with uncertainty, a sense of dis-ease and the feeling of not belonging or not being good enough. Their emotional well-being, necessary for self-esteem and a sense of belonging, all of which are prerequisites to learning, is put under strain. If all children are to learn and succeed, they need to feel safe, secure, valued and included.

Valuing those that care

Historically, caring was seen as the natural work of women: a conflation of mothering and childcare. Today, this is still reflected in attitudes and values in education and society at large – the notion that real learning only starts in school, or that the early years profession does not need to be highly qualified and therefore attracts limited remuneration, leading to some Early Learning and Care (ELC) professionals working for the minimum wage or the living wage.

Until recently the early years sector merited little attention but advances in neuroscience suggest that early neurological windows of opportunity need to be used to advance early learning. This, coupled with the political concept that high quality early years education could provide a better future workforce, has brought the sector under scrutiny, with ever increasing expectations of positive outcomes. Pascal *et al* recently pointed out that 'Investment in the early years sector has the potential to deliver high returns in terms of higher school attainment, reductions in inequality, increased social mobility and enhanced labour market efficiency and capacity.'[7]

Nevertheless, the ELC sector itself remains an outsider within education: undervalued, marginalised and frequently not included, leading to instability in the sector and a high workforce attrition rate.

A unique story

Writing on inclusion, Nutbrown and Clough ask the question: what does 'valuing each child for who they are look like?' They go on to suggest that 'inclusion means different things to different people.'[8] Just as beauty is in the eye of the beholder so too is inclusion and what it means.

Every human being's identity is inextricably bound up with their relationships: there is no one self, for we are in fact many selves. Every human being and living thing that interacts with us sees us differently and uniquely, mirroring back a sense of who we are and where we belong. We slowly come to know ourselves through others and our relationships. ELC professionals are frequently the first to meet children for any considerable length of time outside of their home environment, helping children weave the initial threads of their identity into the wider fabric of society: their life's narrative.

Adults working in ELC have the possibility of granting every child the gift of a reflected self that is unique, loved, positive and valued: the gift of inclusion. To experience a sense of belonging is a critical factor in well-being. As Woodhead and Brooker state, it is the 'psycho-social "glue" that locates every individual. . . and connects people to each other.'[9] They go on to suggest that belonging is 'the relational dimension of personal identity'. To truly belong means that we exist in everyone's minds, thereby creating a warm, inclusive, emotional landscape in which we and our children might grow and thrive.

ELC settings, however, are not neutral places; they are inflected with power and values. A recent report by the Scottish government into the effectiveness of inclusion in Scottish schools notes that not everyone involved with children subscribes to the concept of inclusion. 'Values and beliefs, culture and mind-set are fundamental and there is more work to be done in this regard'. Conversely, many practitioners committed to the principles of including every child are 'disillusioned by the lack of implementation'.[10]

The same report highlights the adverse impact of risk aversion and a 'drive to hit targets' as barriers to successful inclusion, as well as a lack of adequate training and the perception that those working with children who need additional support are under-valued. It highlights the challenge created by the adoption of instrumental practices, with the concomitant need for measure-ment and regulation based on norms, at odds with any pedagogy that promotes child-centred practices and inclusion for all. Instead, the combination of risk aversion, the drive to hit targets and a serious undervaluing of the workforce perpetuates exclusionary practices and the marginalisation of many children who are viewed in terms of deficits instead of strengths.

If practitioners are to meet children's needs, they need to know their children and the best way of doing that is to listen and observe them keenly, sensitively and without judgement. 'Because inclusive *policies* are, in fact, only realised in acts of inclusive *practices*, *what* happens and *how* children are enabled to *belong* are crucial'.[11]

Supporting inclusion for all

Children need time – their time – in which to be, to explore, to grow, to feel, to ponder, to question, to play, to wonder. Keri Opai, a Maori strategic lead in mental health, addiction and disability has ascribed the word Takiwātanga to those with autism, meaning 'in my/his/her own time and space'. He drew inspiration from the tītoki tree 'that does not fruit regularly but does it in its own time, an allusion to autistic people blooming in their own time and space.'[12] Takiwātanga, however, is a word I would use to support all children in their development and to uphold every child's right to be included, as giving children the time they need is a sure sign of respect, understanding and knowing each child's needs.

However, to uphold every child's right to be included, respected and nurtured, practitioners need to be open and non-judgemental in their relationships with the children in their care. As Nutbrown suggests, practitioners need 'wide eyes and open minds'[13] to which I add warm hearts and a strong foundation in our professional abilities.[14] This is the practice of 'attentive love'.[15] For many practitioners, however, this may feel threatening, leading them to ask, 'What's love got to do with it? I'm here to teach.'

Children who learn in different ways challenge our understanding of who we are as practitioners and what we know. To accommodate all children's needs, practitioners have to examine their own views, values and assumptions and this can be uncomfortable, or distressing.

Practitioner identity stands at the intersection of individual values, beliefs and habits, and policy guidelines, society's mores, values and the current political context. To achieve inclusion therefore as practitioners we need to be bold and courageous; willing to challenge ourselves, willing to change; willing to know ourselves inwardly as well as how we engage with the world. This is no mean feat and asks that early years professionals are alert, reflective and responsive in their work. . . all for low wages and within a sector that is undervalued. This is a matter that needs redress, urgently, for ELC practitioners have the responsibility of removing barriers to participation to create a more just, inclusive and equitable society at the beginning of children's lives, while themselves working in a sector that is marginalised.

A pandemic pause: time to reflect

The Scottish mace is inscribed with the words *wisdom, justice, compassion* and *integrity* – values intended to reflect the aspirations of the Scottish people. In ELC we need to be compassionate towards the children in our care and to be just in upholding their rights. We also need to develop wisdom to understand our children deeply and to work with integrity to ensure all children are included.

A well-known philosophical question asks us to consider, 'If a tree falls down in the forest when no-one is there, does it make a sound?' Ears can hear and eyes can see but, if no-one witnesses the fall or the sound, where does it exist? Did it happen?

If a child calls out and no-one is there who is willing to listen or to see, how does that child know they exist? Inclusion, to me, means living and working intentionally – willing to hear and see every child, to help them feel a sense of belonging, to feel included.

As a result of COVID-19, human beings have the opportunity to step back, think and reflect. For many, the silence and isolation brought the importance of relationships, love and acts of kindness to the fore. In giving consideration to all matters ELC, now is the time to reflect, reconsider and reimagine what ELC and the early years of childhood are all about. It's time to put relationships, love and well-being centre-stage and to recalibrate our bearings for a better, healthier, more sustainable and inclusive future. 'Radical kindness demands institutional change'[16] but there is no time like the present in which to consider such a change.

Endword

Some time ago I attended the graduation ceremony of Aidan and Malek. As they each stepped up to take their award scroll, I was reminded of the hesitant, anxious, courageous, powerful children that had been in my care. I reflected on the fact that they had actually been my teachers, helping to challenge my assumptions and beliefs, causing me sleepless nights and much concern but consequently making me a better human being. They taught me that time, play and the space in which to simply be and belong are critical and invaluable factors in every young child's developing life-narrative. *They taught me the meaning and power of inclusion.* □

SECTION TWO

How can we get to where we want to be?

This section looks at the practicalities of introducing a kindergarten stage in Scotland within the next few years:

■ Lisa McCabe, early years lead for Falkirk, describes how her local authority introduced rights-focused, relationship-centred, play-based education across the three to seven age range (using 'Play is the Way' as their slogan).

■ Sarah Latto, manager of Scotland's ground-breaking Secret Garden outdoor nursery, describes how her setting supports every aspect of early child development, and how it currently offers kindergarten care and education for children aged three to seven.

■ Patricia Anderson and Diane Delaney, co-founders of the parents' organisation Give Them Time, describe their campaign for four-year-olds to be automatically allowed a further year of nursery care and how they achieved a promise to change the law.

■ Sue Palmer, literacy specialist, explains how a 'kindergarten approach' lays sound foundations for reading and writing. . . and can also help close the poverty-related attainment gap.

■ Juliet Robertson, author of *Messy Maths*, explains the advantages of a developmental approach (including outdoor play) for maths teaching and learning that has lifelong benefits.

■ Professor Aline-Wendy Dunlop, Dr Marion Burns and Dr Lynn McNair use their vast shared practical experience to recommend ways of raising the status of the early years workforce, across the current nursery/primary school divide.

■ A nursery teacher and a former primary head teacher – Kate Johnston and Sue Palmer – outline the next steps in 'realising the ambition' for a Scotland-wide kindergarten stage (three to seven) despite the barriers to such a significant culture change.

Chapter 6
Realising 'Realising the Ambition': leading play pedagogy in a local authority

Lisa McCabe

THE EARLY LEVEL in Scotland's Curriculum for Excellence is designed to unify young children's experiences and outcomes across two sectors: early learning and childcare and early primary. This should leave us in no uncertain terms about how the under-sevens should experience their formative years in school. Yet, for seasoned campaigners like myself, it still feels like there's too much variation in perspective about whether play should be the chosen pedagogy in every P1 classroom.

I'm not aiming in this chapter to present the convincing arguments for play-based pedagogy. Rather I hope to take a more optimistic standpoint underpinned by the belief that in recent years the teaching community in Scotland has evolved from a position of play-neutrality to one of play-enthusiasm.

But how did we get there? And where is 'there'?

Three key drivers for change

In my current role as Education Team Manager in Falkirk, I'm often asked the question: 'What has accounted for the success?' I fear my response undoubtedly falls short of being compelling. On reflection, presenting a recipe for success is challenging because the factors involved are multi-faceted and contextual –

it's difficult to cite one thing or one defining moment.

Success always relies on the contribution of others, the people involved. Context is always important too. Local authorities have differing priorities, unique to them, and this creates its own complexity. Writing this chapter has provided an opportunity to reflect deeply on 'what works' in delivery of play pedagogy in my own local authority system.

I am sure of one thing: Scotland's early childhood education (ECE) approach is suffering from something of an identity crisis. If it weren't, there would be no need for the present level of debate. So for those of us who have a clear vision of ECE in our local context, realising the vision requires the deliberate, relentless 'conscious cultivation' of these three drivers:

1. Highly effective system leadership.

2. Entitlement to systemic practical support for teachers.

3. Parents as advocates for play.

Presenting these as necessary drivers doesn't mean I am basking in success, having attended to each fully. There is always more to do. I have learned from many colleagues across Scotland who have offered me counsel and the comfort of knowing that I'm not alone in my pursuit. So, for the remainder of the chapter, I will take each of the three drivers and offer thoughts and reflections, drawing upon my own context, in the hope of being helpful to others as others have been to me.

1. Highly effective system leadership

Thanks to *Realising the Ambition,* Scotland's early childhood education (ECE) system is in the process of transformational change. While this is to be welcomed and embraced, we must recognise the biggest pitfall of all: the perception that such transformation can be *quickly* embedded. It cannot. To entertain the notion that simply declaring 'we do play' – without proper attention to issues of quality, sustainability and longevity – will serve only to destabilise the system for no apparent gain.

Leadership for lasting transformation

To avoid this, it is important that all levels of the system understand from the outset the rationale for embarking on this journey of transformational change. All parts of the system must know their part and play it well and convincingly. Everyone has to accept that the pace will undulate over time, with phases of intensity followed by fallow periods where there is ostensibly 'nothing to see here'.

Above all else, this is a long game we are playing (no pun intended). The pursuit of quick results, in whatever terms those are, would skew the narrative to one of compliance over purpose. I feel strongly that those upon whom our nation's success relies, our teachers, need to be protected from the distraction of haste.

Rushing teachers into adopting play pedagogy is harmful because it undermines the purpose. Over my career, I've often been asked 'When will we have this sorted?' My response is: 'Do you want this done quickly or do you want it done properly?' It is the same for teachers, and those in a leadership position should account for that in planning.

In practical terms, the articulation of clear and explicit aims, outcomes and actions throughout all layers of strategic planning helps safeguard against superficial compliance or the idea that this is simply an on-trend development. Play pedagogy is not a fashion nor is it 'of the moment'. It is based on international research and informed by neuroscience. The system right now appears riper than ever for this change and we shouldn't create the notion that we are simply 'giving it a go for now'.

The language of leadership
Clever strategic planning, articulated well, seeks not permission but sets out intention. The job of officers is to know and understand the 'why'. When that is understood, the language used to frame strategic plans sets the tone. Terminology associated with newness, trialling or testing misrepresents the basis upon which the plan is formed. To support colleagues in our schools, the language must convey a more assured stance.

Language is always important. We often use the word 'play' as shorthand for 'a developmentally appropriate approach to the curriculum, learning and teaching'. And how could anyone object to that? The alternative is an un-developmental, in-appropriate approach! I suspect there wouldn't be much support for that amongst system leaders.

However, the use of 'play' does somewhat split the crowd. It is a lay term and everyone has their own definition. So should we change to 'play pedagogy'? Drop 'play' from the rhetoric altogether? Or stick with 'play' and create an operational definition that is well understood?

In Falkirk, we stuck with 'play'. We're in this for the long game and can't keep having this 'to play or not to play' debate. We must grasp it, define it for our purpose and be confident about it. If permission is needed, we don't need to look very far in our national guidance where 'play' is used repeatedly.

Falkirk achieved its quest for an operational definition through creation of a brand: *Play is the Way*. This visible branding provided opportunities to talk about play confidently and unashamedly. The 'drip drip' effect of seeing the phrase *Play is the Way*, accompanied by the operational definition appearing in all plans, brought about a credible actuality and a compelling sense of inevitability. Above all, it helped those to whom it matters feel part of something very significant. I've learned to my delight that, in a transformational development driven by those closest to the change – our school leaders and teachers – it becomes very difficult for any stakeholder who is slightly removed to be anything other than supportive.

I have also found that, subtle though it is, the shift of language to 'improvement' rather than 'change' helps enormously. A rhetoric of change conveys experimentation and gives rise to concern that post-change will be new and unknown. By contrast, improvement is not wholesale abandonment but targeted at addressing aspects of practice that work less well for children. Who would argue against that?

Leadership for staged improvement
My aim as a system leader has been to establish play pedagogy – *Play is the Way* – as the norm. In so doing, it helped to think about the system as needing to move through a series of stages:

- Transition into *Play is the Way*

- Embedding of *Play is the Way*

- Sustaining *Play is the Way*

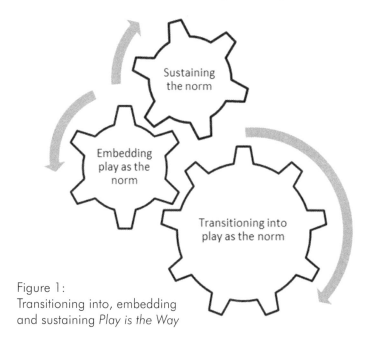

Figure 1:
Transitioning into, embedding
and sustaining *Play is the Way*

My perspective just now is that of a system leader at a local authority level but I believe this phasing applies equally to a school or even to an individual teacher. Whatever the perspective, explaining the systemic approach in this way conveys its longevity. This guards against any idea that play pedagogy can be passed off as a twinkly 'here for now' initiative.

Planning also requires a firm idea of what differentiates the stages and clarity about what it takes to get from one stage to the next. It is important to understand that each stage requires a significant investment of time, effort and resource. All these investments need to be thoughtful, deliberate and equitable over time.

I have a nagging concern that if Scotland remains for very much longer in the transition stage, history will repeat itself and we'll have delivered yet another failed revolution.

The success of Falkirk's *Play is the Way* brand is characterised by broad acceptance amongst all parties that play pedagogy is 'what we do here'. For me, this shows that the strategic planning and system leadership have worked. Indeed, I believe we are now coming out of the transition phase and entering the stage of normalisation.

But it would be extreme folly to think there is no more work to do. The normalising phase is arguably even more challenging. There's no big bang; no fanfare; no bells and whistles. Simply, in a normalised phase, play pedagogy is now the everyday way of working – there is nothing that separates *Play is the Way* from any other part of the system. So, the question for me, and for others at the same stage, is: how do you capitalise on the energy created in the transition phase to build-up momentum that will sustain play as the norm?

2. Entitlement to systemic practical support for teachers

Each stage needs investment and nourishment and this involves the systemisation of practical support. I believe that, for the system to move through the stages, a robust framework of support for teachers is necessary, spanning initial teacher education through probationer support and on to career-long professional learning.

In Falkirk, our *Play is the Way* message is firmly embedded in our probationer programme each year, providing the opportunity to share the strategic expectations with new colleagues who may or may not be teaching at the early stages. Feedback is always positive. The experience of the head teachers and teachers who deliver the programme achieves for us the essence of what this section is all about: practical support. Our in-service teachers and leaders have benefited from a myriad of support, ranging from expert tutelage from prominent thinkers in the field to the offer of regular and planned support from local networks of peers.

Despite considerable investment in high quality professional learning opportunities at local level, my colleagues have shown that there is no such thing as 'too much' when it comes to practical support and learning. The level of uptake of learning opportunities, including evenings and weekends, highlights a need which will be long lasting. These teachers are consummate professionals who understand their accountabilities and are serious about delivering the best education they can for children. This, I am sure, is reflected in every authority across Scotland.

In pursuit of the new normal, I find it unpalatable that local authorities should be forced to compete as to who wins the best professional advice for teachers. A national framework, delivered locally, and lasting at least a generation, tailored to the unique contribution role teachers make in delivering a play pedagogy, would undoubtedly move the system at pace out of transition and into a normalised phase which feels natural and accepted.

3. Parents as advocates for play

Scottish parents have a high degree of faith in our education system. While issues inevitably arise in school that require mediation and resolution, I have found these are seldom directly concerned with curriculum or pedagogy. By and large, parents trust teaching professionals to design and deliver learning to achieve their desired outcome.

But how do parents gauge their level of satisfaction with their child's school? In my experience they care most about their child's happiness, friendships, motivation for learning, attitude to school and relationship with the teacher. When dissatisfaction occurs it is usually because something is amiss in one or more of these areas. Often the problem does actually stem from issues to do with curriculum and pedagogy: learning is too hard or too easy; the child is in the wrong reading group; teaching style does not suit, and so on.

It therefore surely follows that a pedagogy which is child-centred, relationship-based and capitalises on the child's motivations and dispositions, would serve to prevent these initial seeds of unhappiness or dissatisfaction from occurring. A pedagogy which values not only curriculum outcomes, but children's motivation, independence, social well-being and self-regulation. In short, a developmentally-sensitive, holistic pedagogy where children learn how to learn. This is what you get with play pedagogy.

Has COVID affected parents' perceptions?

As I write, we are in the middle of the global COVID-19 pandemic. The closure of schools and nurseries in Scotland thrust parents – without warning or preparation – into the role of home-learning facilitators. In an effort to support families, I spoke to several groups of parents whose children would be going into Primary 1. I was anxious to gain insight as to their hopes and fears, particularly as the usual transition activities would not be possible.

During the exchanges, parents were open and honest. Although clearly drawing from a range of experiences and circumstances, they were broadly similar in their aspirations for their young children as they entered school. They wanted their child to be regarded uniquely, with well-being prioritised above all else. Without exception, they wanted their child to be happy, contented and nurtured when in school.

Some parents worried that their child might not be ready for school and discussion took us into the interesting subject of 'school readiness'. I hate that terminology and have never subscribed to it – and parents in my groups, after discussing together, seemed not to subscribe to it either. My preference is to think more of 'ready schools', where the starting point for children is neither pre-empted nor prescribed.

Indeed, to revisit my opening remarks about the Early Level and its purpose, there is surely a dichotomy here. If – as should be the case – parents understood the purpose of the Early Level, 'school readiness' would be eliminated from their consciousness. I am afraid the fact they raised it at all means there's more to be done to bring about shared vision and purpose with all stakeholders, especially parents.

In non-pandemic circumstances, parents' questions about moving to primary school are normally practical questions about the playground, lunch hall, what to bring, what to wear, etc. But these issues were less relevant to parents who had been exposed to media reports of children having to 'socially distance' from peers, being unable to share learning materials and resources, confined to an assigned desk and chair with limited movement for the majority of the day. These thoughts seemed to horrify them. They did not want that for their young children, nor could they conceive it.

One parent remarked, 'Falkirk is all about play in Primary 1. I am really worried that my child will miss out on that.' Joy! A parent advocating for play!

A parental culture change?

Interestingly, not one person in the group disagreed. It seemed they all were drawing comfort from the idea of a play-based curriculum for their children. For me, this represented a highly significant development in the quest to move from convincing to conviction. It seemed that, without trying or being asked to, parents had moved from a position of simply 'going with it' to one of *advocating* for a play approach above any other.

The group dynamic was interesting. The level of conviction about play (and how this was the way they wished their young child to experience their learning) expressed by a few parents was compelling. So compelling, in fact, that it served to convince those who perhaps would have been as easily swayed in another direction had a counter-response been offered.

I don't think parents in the group realised the profound effect their words and actions on that day had on me. The discussion completely changed my own thoughts about the role of parents in achieving this transformational ambition we have for play as the cornerstone of our system for early childhood education in Scotland.

But what had accounted for the shift?

I am not sure I know the answer definitively and it's worth further exploration. My thoughts so far are that the attitudinal change in those parents arose from their experience, during lockdown, in having a changed role as educator of their child. They now, it seemed to me, had insight as to how their young child learns best and, equally, they had an acute sense of what represented less than effective approaches.

During the discussion, a few parents shared the benefit of their hindsight, giving examples of the pitfalls of attempting to get their child 'to sit down and do their letters and numbers' or presenting tasks for their child to do while their child had a different idea or plan. There were nods of agreement. It was becoming clear that having acquired a level of insight as to how their child thinks and behaves as a learner, they were firmly of the view that a traditional idea of schooling would be futile at best in achieving the ambitions they had for their children at school.

These parents had passion and conviction. Their sense of relief was palpable when I explained that play pedagogy is 'what we do here'. For me, until now, parents were a group that needed to be convinced. Clearly, through the excellent work done by schools and teachers in Falkirk in that regard, there is remarkable potential amongst parents to lead the system into the new normal and it will be my next endeavour to ensure that this is the case.

Conclusion

Writing this chapter has provided me with the opportunity to share my thinking about what it takes at a system level to establish play as the mainstay of our nation's ECE identity.

To have an identity is all-important as it brings about a level of consciousness about what we do and why we do it. We look outwards and admire the strong and identifiable ECE brands in other countries around the world. However, we are, I believe on the brink of something monumental in Scotland: a whole system movement, which, led with conscious positivity and credibility at national and local levels, will provide all Scottish children with the very best possible start to their education. □

Chapter 7
A kindergarten stage at the Secret Garden

Sarah Latto

THE SECRET GARDEN Outdoor Nursery opened its invisible doors back in 2008. As one of the UK's first fully outdoor children's nurseries it has been a pioneer setting in Early Learning and Childcare (ELC). The nursery – which is near the village of Letham in Fife – was the long-held vision of its founder, Cathy Bache. Cathy saw a different approach to education in the early years, one which was rich with song, community, play and nature. She saw the Secret Garden as being more than 'just' a nursery, instead an experiential community, creating a different way of being in the world. The Secret Garden community creates new values and attitudes which resonate wholly with the natural world. In Cathy Bache's words these are:

> Nature being fully recognised as the most pivotal and fundamental aspect of our lives. Without Nature, the elements, the cycles and rhythms of the year we could not exist on this planet.

Nature pedagogy
At its core, the Secret Garden (near Letham in Fife) has three guiding principles; Presence, Nature and Play. The three principles are what guide our everyday activities, they nurture us and inspire us, allowing us to be the best that we can be for the children in our care.

Presence is what grounds us. To have a calm mind, to allow yourself to be in the moment, to truly arrive each morning and connect with yourself and colleagues. This is how practitioners begin their day in the woods. The 'tune-in' is what we call it, ten minutes dedicated to just 'arriving'. It may focus on movement or meditation, to help us feel the earth below us, hear the wind in the trees or the smell of the rain, to feel sun on skin, to awaken the senses and allow the mind to arrive with the body, united together, here, ready for the day ahead. In the woods, practitioners aim to hold on to that sense of groundedness, as it is only by being present ourselves that we can be present for the children.

There is a certain magic that happens in the woods, when practitioners are able to stand back and let Nature take her lead as teacher. Practitioners create and hold a space for the children to feel free, to explore and follow their curiosities while feeling safe and connected with the adults around them. In these magic moments, we see the unfolding of potential, witness the development of learning, watch children as they try, test, succeed and fail. All as part of the learning journey, of that serious business of play. Presence represents a mindfulness of practitioners in the woods, a commitment to the children by being a caregiver who is wholly there in body and in mind, actively holding the space, being respectful of the children, aware and ready to respond if required.

Practitioners are recognised as facilitators at Secret Garden: Nature is the teacher. Our 'Spiral Curriculum' uses symbols from the natural world to associate with areas of learning and development. Learning outcomes are symbolized by trees on the Confident Happy Child and by a range of nature symbols on the Inspired Creative Child spiral. We are immersed in Nature everyday at Secret Garden and we use an eco-vocabulary in our daily discussions about what we see happening around us. We are based entirely out-of-doors (with the exception of our yurt shelter) all year round and so the children have the wonderful opportunity to experience the changing seasons in all their glory. They return home at the end of the day with tales of being intrepid explorers, with stories of exhilaration, awe and survival!

Learning through play, outdoors all day

Visitors often remark on the resilience of the Secret Garden children. This resilience comes from learning to maintain one's equilibrium, to remain in balance no matter what the weather (or other areas of life!) might throw at you. Our practitioners see 'adverse' weather as an opportunity, responding to the children's inquisitive nature as they follow little streams and collect rain drops. Building dens and coorying in to listen to the wind howling around, or building fires and singing songs to keep spirits high on snowy days.

Our Training Facilitator, Louise Durrant, puts it beautifully:

> For sure we need to be alert to the dangers. But there is also a danger of over-protection. Children (and adults) need to fully experience the weather, to feel the power of the elements and how they shape the environment, how they move and shape us. We too are wild in our hearts and souls. Let the children feel the wildness of the weather as a call and response to their own wonderful wildness, the vitality that we never want to tame.

This different way of being in the world recognizes that we are all a part of this beautiful planet. And the Secret Garden children grow into custodians of the woods, developing their own environmental identities. The richness of the time and space they are offered at Secret Garden soon fosters this within them, as they grow in a sense of belonging with Nature, feeling a deep sense of connection and groundedness.

Within this mindfully held space, in the natural environment of the woods, the Secret Garden children can experience truly free play. Everything is set up to allow this. The unhurried atmosphere, the songful transitions, group stories, lunch and snack circles and end of day reflections all support a fluid movement from one stage of the day to the next. The woods themselves also support play as each site has clearly distinguishable features which make it unique: the Moon Den, the Cooking Tree, Where the Dragons Live, the Tree with the Hole, all beautifully named by the children because of the playful possibilities they hold.

Within the natural environment of the woods, children are able to find multitudes of different ways to play. A giant stump becomes a helicopter landing pad, an upturned tree root becomes a family car, a small tree is transformed into an ice-cream shop, witches fly around on broomsticks and make potions out of mud and pine cones, and a little den is where a family of tigers sleep. The loose parts provided by the woods are all the children need to be inspired, curious and motivated learners. Some simple materials and resources are on offer: baskets, chalk, rope, ID guides, etc. However for the most part, children find everything that they need from the natural environment for a rich and immersive day of play with peers.

Our kindergarten stage

Since 2018 the Secret Garden has been running a group for

older children (up to age seven) as part of the daily nursery group. Known as the Buzzards (key groups at Secret Garden are animals/birds) this group came about due to enquiry and interest from parents. There was a real appetite and longing from parents to have the option of their child remaining at Secret Garden into their fifth and sixth year. Historically there had been a few cases when an older child had deferred entry to school and remained with the nursery for an extra year but this was the first time where we had an older group remaining on together.

After consultations with interested parents, practitioners and directors, the consensus was clear and we set about creating a pilot study, offering a group of children the opportunity to remain at the Secret Garden for another year. Their parents applied to the primary school for permission to 'flexi-school' (which means children attend school for some days of the week, while being home-schooled or attending alternative educational provision on the other days). Some head teachers are more on board with this than others, but we supported the applications by talking to the teachers concerned and eight went through. Throughout the pilot study we had regular parent meetings, discussions with the children in the woods and feedback from practitioners working with the children. We learnt a lot!

Originally we had the idea, following parent preferences, that the Buzzards would all attend on the same day so that they had peers of a similar age within their group. Parents also liked the idea of an increase in 'activities' – perhaps more time off in their own Buzzard group with a practitioner where focused tasks could take place: cooking, group den building, nature crafts etc. were all offered. But practitioners soon discovered that the dynamic of taking the group out and then reintroducing them upset the flow of the day for all children. And after a while the Buzzards lost interest in 'going off' and wanted to remain a core part of the main group. It was easy for us to understand why – they still enjoyed playing with the younger children.

It suddenly became very clear what the Buzzards were craving. They needed their time in the woods to be free and spacious, exactly as it had been before. They needed time to play. Some would arrive on a Thursday morning, all wound-up and hyper, buzzing about and talking nonstop. Then, by mid-morning they were calmer, more focused, able to listen and respond, valuing and respecting their peers, finding their selves again.

Three- to seven-year-olds, learning together

Once we realized that this model of all being together in the one group was what worked best for the children, we really began to notice the benefits of having a mixed age group in the woods. Over the years we have witnessed the Buzzards acting as role models, stepping up to offer help, keeping the peace or offering solutions to support the younger children. We have observed younger children seeking out the older ones for help, to read to them or to play, drawn to their abilities and social skills to create complex games and to keep the games going, managing any upsets and being inclusive.

Of course there were times when the Buzzards enjoyed sitting on a blanket or hanging in a tree with a couple of friends and did not want to be interrupted by an eager three-year-old. But the diversity of the woodland environment allows for this, providing enough space, enough hidey holes, or high up branches for the older ones to access for a bit of space and time together.

Practitioners also noticed that the Buzzards, due to their increased time spent at Secret Garden, were very well- practised in the ways and routines of the day which proved to be extremely helpful in supporting the younger children. If a new child was perhaps venturing too far away we would hear a voice calling 'Hey, come back! You have to stay together!' On one occasion, someone was over eager to get back to playing and forgot to pack away her lunch and we witnessed a group of Buzzards discussing what was best – for them to pack away the child's lunch for her, or to go and get the child and bring her back so she could do it herself. The group decided on the latter and supported her to pack away her lunchbox and then decided to play together. No adult intervention was required.

Today (2020) we have about ten Buzzards who attend on various days at Secret Garden, allowing a lovely mix of ages on most days in the woods. Although we do find Thursdays and Fridays are preferable days for those children who are flexi-schooling, those who are home-schooling have a bit more flexibility. Due to their age, the Buzzards do not receive council funding and so most of the Buzzards only attend one day per week. We do have a couple who now attend two days as Buzzards and we are aware that some would attend more days if funding was available.

Over the years the Buzzards have become an integral part of nursery life. They have a unique identity and many of the young children aspire to become Buzzards when they are old enough. As practitioners we see the real benefits, academic and social, of allowing children that extra year or two, to remain free in the woods for that little while longer.

Conclusion

To sum up, the Secret Garden is currently operating as a part-time kindergarten, and has been since 2018. We have witnessed first hand the rich learning opportunities and supportive social benefits that come with children interacting in a natural environment in mixed age groups. We hope that this model of ELC may be offered to more children over the years to come and would be delighted to support any setting who would like to explore the possibilities. ☐

Chapter 8
Parent Power: how a grass-roots campaign secured a promise to change the law

Patricia Anderson and Diane Delaney,
co-founders of the Give Them Time campaign

SCOTLAND'S very early school starting age can cause particular problems for the youngest children in a 'school age group' who are only four years old when they move up from nursery into school. In most countries of the world this doesn't happen until children are six or seven years old, so four is exceptionally young for the transition and many parents feel it will be detrimental for their child.

In May 2018 we set up the Facebook group 'Deferral Support Scotland'[1] with the aim of providing parents with a clear understanding of their legal right to defer school entry for any child not age five by start of the school year in Scotland.[2] We also hoped that, as membership increased, parents could be put in touch with others in the same local authority area who had either been through the process of deferring their child there or who were also embarking on that journey. To date (July 2020) we have almost 2700 members and 31 associated local area messenger chat groups.

Why was there a need for such a support group?
Before Deferral Support Scotland was set up, many parents looking for support and advice about deferring their child's start

in Primary 1 discovered the Upstart Scotland movement, which calls for a kindergarten stage for three- to seven-year-olds, based on the successful Nordic models. While Upstart's aspiration chimed with many of these parents' views about their child's development in terms of them being more likely to thrive in a formal learning environment at a later stage, this was a long-term solution which wouldn't help their own four-year-old now.

However, inevitably many discussions around the issue of deferral in Scotland arose on Upstart's Facebook threads with, despite the best of intentions, mixed advice being given due to the law on this area not being well known or easily accessible and practices varying in each local authority area.

Most commenters seemed to know that a January- or February-born child could be deferred but what was less well understood was that a child with a birthday between mid-August (the start of the new school year) and 31 December also has a legal right to start primary school aged five instead of aged four in Scotland, if their parents/carers choose this for them.

If parents were fortunate enough to have found out about their legal right to defer their mid-August to 31 December-born child, they then had to find out what the process was for applying for a further year of funded nursery in their local authority area. Scotland has had a 99 per cent uptake of funded three-to five-year old nursery places in recent years so this was an issue for the vast majority of parents looking to defer their child's start in Primary 1. Whilst parents have the legal right to choose deferral for their four-year-old, their local authority can make it incredibly difficult for them to do so, as they can refuse both the funding for that continued nursery place *and* the parent's choice to self-finance a further year of nursery for their child at a local authority nursery – even if space is available for the child to remain there.

These details were fairly unknown and hence the decision was made to set up the Deferral Support Scotland Facebook group to provide a one-stop shop for accurate information on this.

The evolution of the Give Them Time Campaign

After just three weeks of the setting up of the Facebook group, the Give Them Time campaign emerged from it. As parents shared their experiences of being misinformed about their rights, being subjected to wildly different application processes and the likelihood of funding being greater in some local authorities than others, it became clear that this was a national injustice which had to be challenged and that a co-ordinated approach to doing so was required. A survey collated parents' experiences more formally and this enabled the campaign's founders to identify the key issues they were experiencing across the country. From these, the campaign made it its mission to call for a more transparent, consistent and child-centred approach to be taken by local authorities when considering funding requests for a child's deferral year in nursery.

From claims to credibility

Our argument initially was based on anecdotal evidence but we realised that, to be taken seriously, we needed credibility. We sought to establish this by submitting Freedom of Information requests to all 32 local authorities in order to determine the truth about their deferral funding application processes and approval rates.

We designed a campaign logo and our next step was to spread the word to parents. This was done by asking supporters to share information on various parent-interest Facebook groups and by setting up a campaign Twitter account. We also sought to garner support from relevant children's and parents' groups.

By the time of the campaign's launch event in Edinburgh on 6th November 2018, the former Children and Young People's Commissioner, Tam Baillie, had become an official supporter and seven national organisations, or their senior staff, had done likewise. These were Children in Scotland, the parent-teacher organisation Connect, Director of Scotland Home-Start UK, National Parent Forum of Scotland, Play Scotland, Reform Scotland and Upstart Scotland.

Research findings

In early autumn 2018 the National Parent Forum of Scotland conducted a national survey on our behalf about parents' knowledge of which children had a right to be deferred. It consolidated our expectations by showing that of the 559 respondents representing all thirty-two local authority areas, 80 per cent knew of the right to defer a January- or February-born child but only 16 per cent knew that an August- to December-born child had the same entitlement.

The responses to our Freedom of Information requests also supported what parents had said when sharing their experiences on the Facebook group and proved that not only did funding application processes for a deferral year in nursery vary widely by local authority area but the likelihood of gaining this funding also varied.

Other research conducted by the campaign to establish a fuller picture of the discrepancies across the country revealed a wide variation in the information available on councils' websites about the right to defer this autumn-born cohort. Some websites didn't refer to it at all, others stated that children born between September and December could be deferred (completely omitting mid/late August-born children). Further confusion was also often created by the language used on such webpages, because many councils referred to the right to apply for deferral for mid-August to December-born children without distinguishing between a parent's right to defer such a child and the local authority's right to decide whether to fund a further year of nursery for them or not.

We launched a website[3] along with the campaign on 6th November 2018 and the evidence section contains the campaign's most up-to-date research findings.

Next steps
Our next steps involved meeting with the Convention of Scottish Local Authorities (COSLA) and the Minister for Children and Young People, Maree Todd, to discuss our research findings and the ongoing issues parents were facing when trying to use their legal right to defer their child. COSLA agreed to discuss our concerns at their Children and Young People's Board and Ms Todd agreed to review the Ministerial guidance local authorities use to make these funding decisions.

While we were pleased with the interest and engagement from local and national government as well as some media attention, none of these was resolving parents' difficulties or the postcode lottery of inequality quickly enough.

In April 2019 COSLA's Children and Young People's Board (comprised of the chairs of each Scottish local authority's Education Committee) agreed that local authorities would take a more consistent approach to ensuring greater clarity on deferral rights in all of their communications with parents on this issue. Specifically they would make it clear that any child not age five by the school commencement date could be deferred and also that there was a distinction between a parent's legal right to choose deferral and a council's right to refuse continued nursery funding for a deferral year for a non-January/ February-born child.

The Give Them Time campaign welcomed this decision but felt it did not go far enough to resolve the unfairness that some local authorities continued to have a 100 per cent approval rate of granting this funding whereas others approved fewer than 50 per cent of such requests. **It was the view of parents that there was a conflict of interest within local authorities with their staff having the role of managing capacity in their nurseries whilst also being the decision makers in approving funding for deferral (or not). This conflict does not exist for parents as they only act in the best interests of their child.**

Following the COSLA agreement a parliamentary members' debate took place in Holyrood on 1st May 2019 which demonstrated cross-party support for the campaign. We were delighted that the issue had been discussed on the national stage but sadly it was anti-climactic as there was still no appetite from the government to change the law, despite sweeping agreement from the various parties' speakers.

A more local approach

Between May and September 2019 there was more activity at local level where the power still lay in making these funding decisions. Parents in various areas wrote to their local councillors which led to the issue being debated at three local authority full council meetings. Elected members at all of these voted on whether to change to an automatic funding policy for a further year of nursery for all children whose parents chose to take up their legal right to defer their P1 start. However, the vote was lost in Fife and East Renfrewshire Councils, and despite it being unanimously supported in North Lanarkshire in June 2019, the policy decision was subsequently overturned there in February 2020 before it had even had a chance to be implemented. We were bitterly disappointed and resolved that the only solution now would be a national one as the local approach was not productive.

An unexpected announcement

On 2nd October 2019, Scottish Labour chose the issues raised by the campaign as the focus of their education debate at the Scottish Parliament. This time, unlike at the members' debate in May, MSPs would vote on their views at the end of the afternoon's presentations. As we had hoped, the contributions from various MSPs were overwhelmingly supportive of the campaign's calls and during the debate, the Minister for Children and Young People stated that she would introduce legislation to fund a further year of nursery for all children legally deferring.

This was completely unexpected as she had previously focused her efforts on rewriting the guidance for local authorities on this issue. In addition, at the end of the debate the majority of

MSPs voted in favour of such a law being brought in thus emphasising that the will of parliament should not be ignored.

What next for Give Them Time?

We were delighted by this development but the ongoing battle is now to push for a date for this legislation to be implemented. Progress has been impeded, albeit understandably, due to the government's need to focus on its response to the Covid-19 pandemic in recent months. We remain optimistic that the Minister will follow through on her commitment and that legislation will be brought in before the end of this parliamentary term in 2021 so that parents no longer need to be subjected to arduous, long-winded, professional-heavy application processes in order to be able to use their legal right to defer their child.

The legal right of the parents of any four-year-old in Scotland to defer entry to Primary 1 is absolute. However, their ability to use that right is currently variable, depending on when the child's birthday falls, which local authority area they live in and whether the parents can afford another year of nursery fees if funding is refused. It is unfair that the youngest four-year-olds covered by this law (January- and February-born children) have an automatic entitlement to a further year of nursery funding whilst children born between mid-August and 31 December do not.

With the current 99 per cent uptake rate of the government's free early learning and childcare entitlement, many parents depend on this subsidy to enable them to work and make ends meet. It shouldn't be the case that they have to decide between their child's best interests and whether they can afford to fund a further year of nursery for them. And they certainly shouldn't be forced to move them to another setting entirely if a council thinks they know best.

Is a kindergarten stage the answer?

If Upstart's call for a kindergarten stage for three- to seven-year-olds is successful it would remove the need for the deferral of four-year-olds and all of the difficult issues surrounding this process as described above. There are clearly overlaps in terms of many of the reasons why parents choose to defer their child's primary school start and the child development arguments presented by Upstart e.g. social, emotional, cognitive, behavioural and physical factors.

All of the founding members of the Give Them Time campaign are Upstart Scotland supporters but it would be unfair to simply assume that all of our supporters are too. We are a parents' rights campaign and believe in helping all parents considering deferral to make an informed choice about what is best for their child. It is therefore possible that some are not concerned about the wider social and educational issues around Scotland's early starting age, merely in ensuring their own child's long-term well-being.

However, a distinguishing feature of the parents who support our campaign is that they have, for one reason or another, acquired enough knowledge about child development to make the (often immense) effort to pursue deferral of their child's start at primary school. As other chapters in this book abundantly show, the majority of the population are clearly unaware of the complex nature of early child development and the potential long-term consequences of forcing a child into a formal learning situation before they are ready.

The huge variations of policy we discovered among local authorities suggest there is also a serious lack of knowledge about child development in their education departments, since decisions are frequently taken that serve local bureaucracy's best interest, rather than the best interest of the children.

We are very pleased at the extent to which our campaign has released 'parent power' and brought about a government promise to adjust the law. Until this is achieved, Give Them Time will continue to raise awareness of the problems created by Scotland's extremely early school starting age (and, hopefully, awareness of the science of early child development). And we hope many of our supporters will then join the founders of Give Them Time in working with Upstart Scotland to continue raising public awareness about early child development and eventually establishing a relationship-centred, play-based kindergarten stage for all Scotland's under-sevens. ☐

Chapter 9
Literacy matters . . . but building strong foundations for literacy matters more

Sue Palmer

EVEN in today's multimedia culture, literacy matters. Children who struggle with reading and writing are at a serious disadvantage throughout their schooling and beyond. Not only can literacy difficulties affect career prospects and long-term economic security, they may also have emotional consequences, including low self-confidence and self-image, feelings of disempowerment and, in the long-term, possible mental health problems.[1]

However, despite its fundamental importance, literacy does not 'come naturally' to children. Reading and writing are cultural skills which must be taught. It's therefore essential that primary education systems prioritise literacy acquisition and, for well over a century, literacy specialists have conducted extensive research into the most successful teaching methods.[2]

Teaching literacy – What, how and when?

In countries using alphabetic writing systems, the 'what' of early literacy instruction is now widely agreed to involve:

- the sound-symbol system on which written language depends (phonics)

- the ways in which words are built up (e.g. basic

> phonetic encoding, syllables, morphemic units such as prefixes, suffixes and grammatical chunks like 'ed')
>
> ■ the meaning of written texts (comprehension in reading; composition in writing).

The English language is complex in terms of both phonetic encoding (26 letters representing 44 basic speech sounds) and grammar. Consequently, ever since research into reading instruction began, there's been controversy among literacy specialists about the 'how' of early reading and writing.

Some literacy authorities recommend teachers to concentrate first on systematic teaching of phonics, showing children how to 'decode' and 'encode' words. This method, which is now government policy in England[3], is generally effective in terms of children's immediate performance but not particularly motivating – indeed, in some cases, it's deeply demotivating. And when children don't *want* to read and/or write, they're unlikely to engage in the huge amounts of practice necessary for fluency. So an emphasis on phonics may create readers and writers who are technically competent but not truly literate.

Other literacy specialists urge teachers to create a literacy-rich environment in which children are motivated to start reading and writing for themselves, picking up the necessary knowledge though exposure to print and *ad hoc* adult support.[4] This 'emergent literacy' approach is generally much more motivating than a heavy emphasis on decoding/encoding. Unfortunately, in some cases children fail to pick up the phonic knowledge they need, which again leads to poor literacy outcomes.

Since the advent of national curricula and regular standardised assessment in UK schools, these questions have been settled differently in different parts of the country. In England, the national policy involves heavy emphasis on 'systematic synthetic phonics', while Scotland has opted for a more 'balanced' approach which has, in practice, also involved lots of phonics and handwriting instruction.

So far, however, literacy specialists have given little thought to '**when**' this formal teaching should begin. It is simply assumed that children should start learning to read and write as soon as they enter school.

Too much too soon?

Since universal state schooling began in 1872, Scottish children have started school (and the three Rs) the year they turn five. Most adults in Scotland aren't aware that this is very early indeed. In 66 per cent of countries worldwide the school starting age is six and in 22 per cent it is seven. Only 12 per cent of countries send children to school at four or five (and – largely due to a decision by Westminster politicians in the late 1860s – all bar two are ex-British empire).[5]

In 2004, another generation of Westminster politicians was disappointed that, in the first ever PISA (Programme for International Student Assessment) survey of literacy levels, the UK only came sixth. There had been fierce concentration on literacy teaching in English schools for several years, thanks to heavy investment in a National Literacy Strategy (NLS), so they'd hoped to score higher. Annoyingly, Finland – a country where formal schooling doesn't even start till children are seven – came top of the charts.

As one of the literacy specialists working for NLS, I went to Finland to find out why. . . and discovered that, between the ages of three and seven, children attended a local day-care centre. This provided relationship-centred, play-based 'kindergarten-style' care and education, with a large proportion of the day spent outdoors. During this time, early years practitioners (pedagogues) kept a close watch for any signs of developmental delay and, where there was the slightest concern about a child, immediately consulted with parents. If necessary, specialist help was provided immediately so that the child had every chance to catch up before starting school.

Since Finnish pedagogues also support and encourage 'emergent literacy' (as mentioned above and described in more detail below), most children pick up the basics of reading and writing before the age of seven. Then, when they start school, they're given a formal systematic grounding in phonics/spelling, grammar and handwriting: useful revision for the early starters and a comprehensive introduction for children who haven't previously shown an interest. It's assumed that, by seven, everyone is ready to benefit from formal learning – and specialist help is provided for children who, at any age, do not thrive.

My trip to Finland was life-changing. On return, I gave up specialising in literacy and swapped to studying the intricacies of child development. Everything I've since learned convinces me that, during those four years in developmentally appropriate kindergarten-style settings, Finnish children build sound foundations, not only for the acquisition of literacy skills but also for long-term health and well-being.

In the UK, on the other hand, our very early school starting age has created a cultural expectation of 'too much too soon'.

The rush to teach academic skills at five, four or even (in some nurseries) three not only damages many children's chances of successful literacy acquisition but is probably contributing to developmental disorders and mental health problems in young people.[6]

The foundations of literacy

While literacy does not come naturally to human beings, the foundations upon which literacy is built *do* develop according to a natural blue-print. These foundational skills and capacities are aspects of physical, emotional, social and cognitive development that, over the millennia, have proved beneficial to our species. They develop through a complex interaction between nature (children's individual genetic makeup) and nurture (the caring environment children experience during their early years).

The most obvious underpinning skill is spoken language. Children need a reasonable level of oral fluency and comprehension before they can be expected to transfer these skills into written communication. There's a great deal of research showing that spoken language development depends on positive, supportive relationships with care-givers.[7]

More specific aspects of literacy acquisition depend on the satisfactory development of children's

- auditory discrimination and memory

- phonological awareness (developing implicit awareness of words, syllables, rhyme, initial sounds)

- visual discrimination and memory skills

- pattern recognition (including awareness of letter orientation and directionality)

- hand-eye coordination and small-scale motor skills (which, in turn, depend on large-scale motor skills).

Again, these skills develop naturally through enjoyable interactions with adult carers (including songs, rhymes, language play, music, art and other creative activities), as well as self-directed play.[8]

Memory also plays a critical role in literacy learning. Recall of basic word-level knowledge (e.g. phonics/grammatical chunking /whole-word recognition) must be automatized as quickly as possible, in order to free up working memory for comprehension/composition of meaning.[9] As with all foundational skills, evolution has primed young human beings to develop short and long-term memory skills through supportive 'serve-and-return' interactions with adults and play with their peers.

Finally, successful learning depends on children's 'disposition' towards the task.[10] If young children are highly motivated to acquire a skill, they'll put in immense amounts of practice to consolidate it. But if they're not interested, or pressurised to achieve before developmentally ready to do so, they may become emotionally resistant to the subject.

For the vast majority of children, all the above-listed skills, capacities and dispositions develop during early childhood (defined by the United Nations as birth to age eight) – as long as they're supported by caring, knowledgeable adults and have plenty of opportunities for active, social, self-directed play (as often as possible outdoors). However, literacy researchers tend to concentrate on the development of the specific cognitive skills listed on pages 105/106, which can be taught in isolation, sitting at a desk. Most, therefore, have paid little attention to the holistic mesh of physical, emotional and social development in which these cognitive skills are embedded.

On the other hand, child development researchers pay great attention to the holistic context, particularly to its connection with long-term health, well-being and motivation to learn. They therefore recommend a developmentally appropriate 'emergent literacy' approach to all education, including literacy acquisition, until children are seven years old.[11]

Literacy learning for the under-sevens

After much discussion with colleagues in child development, here's my list of essential requirements for emergent literacy:

A LITERACY-RICH ENVIRONMENT

• frequent sharing of stories and picture books (favourite books over and over again)

• many opportunities for children to create/act out their own stories

• moving to music, singing songs, chanting rhymes

• many opportunities for mark-making, painting, drawing, etc.

• activities that develop hand-eye coordination and small-scale motor control (e.g. cooking, woodwork, sewing, jigsaws, manipulative materials like playdough)

- opportunities to see adults reading and writing **by hand**, for real-life purposes and constant exposure to meaningful, relevant environmental print

- exposure to alphabet letters (song, wall-frieze, fridge-letters, etc.) and – when appropriate – playful introduction to sound/symbol associations

- constant access to reading and writing materials and opportunities to record ideas, e.g. contributing to floor-books

- all the above, underpinned by daily opportunities for 'sustained shared thinking' (talking with peers or adults about events/items of interest)[12] and adult carers who value that communication.

Once children begin to show interest in reading and/or writing for themselves, they usually need support to make further progress. This obviously involves teaching elements of hand-writing, phonics and sentence grammar (e.g. spaces between words and full stops). But for the under-sevens, this teaching should be tailored to individual needs, not standardised expect-ations. It should never be pursued at the expense of overall physical, emotional and social development and no child should be pressurised to learn literacy skills or made to feel inadequate if they are not yet motivated to do so.

Early years practitioners therefore need to be well-informed about early language and literacy acquisition, and ongoing professional development is important. Fortunately, within a developmentally appropriate setting, practitioners' interest in training opportunities is usually high (we have witnessed this in Scotland over recent years as play-based pedagogy grew in popularity; see also Chapter 12). High levels of interest also stimulate practitioner enquiry and action research, leading to innovative projects, such as the Froebel Network's recent work on storytelling in Scotland,[13] which disseminate excellent practice around the profession.

By the age of seven, many – if not most – children raised in such a literacy-rich environment will have begun reading and writing for themselves. After four years of developmentally appropriate care and education, the overwhelming majority will also be sufficiently mature to benefit from formal schooling.

This could begin, as in Finland, with a systematised course in phonics, spelling and handwriting for everyone. On my first visit to Finland (made in the month of September) I asked the teacher of a first grade class 'How long before they're all reading and writing?'

'Oh,' he said casually, 'by Christmas.'

Closing the gap

At present, Scottish educationists are greatly concerned by the gap in educational attainment between children from high- and low-income households (HIHs and LIHs). In terms of vocabulary and problem-solving skills, this gap is already well-established by age three.[14]

Unsurprisingly, most children who show an early interest in reading and writing come from HIHs, where they're more likely to have encountered elements of a 'literacy-rich environment' throughout their early lives than children from less advantaged backgrounds. Three-year-old children from LIHs would clearly benefit from three or four years in a literacy-rich kindergarten, thus levelling the educational playing field. Indeed, I would argue that an emergent literacy approach for the under-sevens would have far more chance of closing the poverty-related attainment gap than Scotland's present policy of assessing specific literacy skills in Primary 1 when children are four or five.

Emergent literacy is a 'bottom-up' holistic developmental process, allowing time for all children to reach their full potential; the Scottish National Standardised Assessment (SNSA) is a 'top-down' academic assessment of specific skills, based on age-related standards. The two approaches are therefore mutually exclusive.

Upstart's many arguments against the P1 SNSA can be found on www.upstart.scot. We are, however, not opposed to assessment *per se* and Chapter 13 of this book suggests an alternative model – assessment of children's overall development, using the Early Development Instrument (EDI). As well as providing data that informs and improves early years support services, in an early-start country like Scotland, substituting the EDI for the P1 SNSA could also transform cultural expectations of early childhood education by highlighting the significance of overall development.

At present, the existence of the P1 SNSA (and its related 'benchmarks' for pupil achievement) means policy-makers at all levels – and the general public – maintain their cultural assumption that teaching of specific literacy skills should begin when children are four or five (Scotland's traditional school starting age). P1 teachers are therefore under pressure to teach these skills. . . and developmentally appropriate practice is thrown to the wind.

The myth of early literacy acceleration

In Chapter 3 of this book, Pam Jarvis explains why authentic learning cannot be 'accelerated' in early childhood. There is, however, no doubt that children can be trained to apply specific literacy skills from the age of four or five – England has proved it for several years with their 'systematic synthetic phonics' instruction towards a national test at age six. It is often justified on the grounds that, English being a phonetically complex language, children need to get started as early as possible in order to cover all the phonic rules.

Specialists in child development, on the other hand, argue that the more complex the symbolic information to be learned, the more sense it makes to wait until children have consolidated all the foundational skills described in the earlier section on *The Foundations of Literacy*. While there may be short-term gains to an earlier start, these appear to be at the expense of long-term damage.

There is, in fact, no evidence that an early start pays any long-term literacy dividends. Sebastian Suggate studied two large cohorts of children in New Zealand: in one, reading instruction began at age five, in the other at age seven.[15] By age eleven, there was no difference in children's reading competence but the early-start group tended to be slightly less motivated and had poorer comprehension than the late starters.

Suggate was looking only at reading outcomes but other long-term studies have considered social and emotional factors. In a USA study of disadvantaged children, Rebecca Marcon[16] found that early formal teaching led to early academic gains but these 'washed out' by the age of ten, and early start children had more emotional and behavioural problems than those who started later.

Extremely long-term studies (e.g. The Perry High/Scope Project[17], covering 25 years and The Longevity Project[18], covering 70 years) show a continuing relationship between an early start on formal learning and later social and emotional problems. These include behavioural and/or learning difficulties during schooling and, in adult life, problems in forging and maintaining relationships that affect employment prospects and family life. The Longevity Project also linked 'too much too soon' to increased mortality, due to health and well-being factors.

The title of a 2013 US research review of the evidence about early formal learning sums it up: 'Little to gain and much to lose.'[19] Indeed, in a culture where children's active, social play is in serious decline, there is more to lose every year. We launched Upstart in 2016 because of mounting concern that the decline of play (especially in the early years) is related to significant increases in children's mental health problems.[20]

Realising the Ambition

Scotland's *Curriculum for Excellence* (*CfE*)[21] aims to develop 'four capacities' in our nation's children – we want them to be 'confident individuals, successful learners, responsible citizens, and effective contributors'. A reasonable level of literacy is, of course, essential to realise all of these. Yet, for the under-sevens, all four capacities are best promoted through relationship-centred, play-based pedagogical practice, not an early concentration on specific cognitive skills.

The 'early level' of *CfE* (for three- to six/seven-year-olds) is based on sound developmental principles, supporting the use of an emergent literacy approach. Unfortunately, for various reasons (not least the cultural assumptions described throughout this book), those developmental principles have not yet been translated into practice in most schools. But the publication of new guidance for Early Level, *Realising the Ambition: Being Me* (2020)[22], is an opportunity to get *CfE* back on track.

The overwhelmingly positive reception for *Realising the Ambition* from across the educational establishment suggests the will is there for transformational change. However, the same educational establishment has been ambivalent about the P1 SNSA, suggesting that most non-early years educators still lack understanding about early child development and believe that, once children reach the school starting age, they're ready to start formal learning.

There is no place in a developmentally appropriate early level for standardised assessment of discrete literacy skills, nor for age-related 'benchmarks' of achievement. Their existence means that many schools still assign P1 children to reading/writing groups based on 'ability' and use reading schemes/programmes in which children progress through numbered or colour-coded levels. All this turns 'the getting of literacy' into a race, in which the acceleration of specific cognitive skills is seen as more important than all-round holistic development (and where HIH children outpace LIH children from the very start).

Literacy matters, but laying sound foundations for literacy matters far more. Scotland's children deserve the 'gift of time' to enjoy their early childhood and also to develop the skills, capacities and disposition to learn on which literacy (as well as other lifeskills, health, well-being and educational success) depends.

Love and play come before formal learning. ☐

Chapter 10
The five Rs of maths: developing a firm mathematical foundation in the early years

Juliet Robertson

I'D LIKE you to imagine a scenario. You are feeling unfit and have decided to join your local gym. You book an initial appointment to have a look round and find out more about what is on offer and the commitment you need to make. When you arrive, you are surprised to see every single person doing press-ups. Some are doing sit-ups too. One or two participants occasionally do a burpee. You turn to the trainer with a quizzical look, 'What's happening here? What about the running, the rowing, the weights and the exercise classes?' you ask.

'Oh, that's no longer our focus,' replies the trainer. 'What matters is press-ups. We need to get everyone to be able to do 100 press-ups. If you can manage 70, we let you move onto sit-ups. Those people doing burpees are particularly fit and able, so that's their extension.'

Now you may not feel you know much about physical fitness but you know enough not to go to that gym. A narrow definition of fitness and limited choices and targets (that's not been designed with you but for you) cannot be described as a motivational or holistic approach to getting fit.

Curiously, the national over-emphasis on attainment in

numeracy and literacy in primary schools is much less questioned as a motivational and holistic approach to providing a high-quality learning environment where children thrive. Children do not grow by being measured, yet our common language around school improvement suggests otherwise as Early Level teachers strive to close 'the attainment gap'.

We have to question whether this 'gap' is an artificial construct. The *Curriculum for Excellence* benchmarks that children are expected to achieve at the end of Primary 1 are remarkably similar to Level A in the *5-14 National Guidance* which stated, 'should be attainable within the course of P1-P3 by almost all pupils.' [1]

Why we need a Five Rs approach

One reason for the increased expectations during the Early Level of *Curriculum for Excellence* is that, as Thiel and Perry point out, there is 'a myriad of studies that seem to show that early childhood mathematics achievement is a strong predictor of success or otherwise in future school mathematics, other school subjects and life itself.' [2]

In 2019, the Education Endowment Foundation (EEF) made five recommendations to support children aged three to seven years to learn maths:

- Develop practitioners' understanding of how children learn maths

- Dedicate time for children to learn mathematics and integrate mathematics throughout the day

- Use manipulatives and representations to develop understanding

- Ensure that teaching builds on what children already know

- Use high-quality targeted support to help all children learn mathematics.[3]

Whilst this looks reasonable (especially as there is no mention of testing children) the challenge is to realise the recommendations in ways which avoid the 'schoolification' of maths, particularly when children move into Primary 1. Phrases such as 'dedicated time' and 'targeted support' are jargon associated with formal approaches. It relies on educators feeling sufficiently confident to interpret this and apply it in a child-centred way.

Our children need to have a strong, broad foundation of maths before formal schooling begins. Maths must be a normal everyday occurrence that happens through thoughtful interactions, joyful experiences in spaces that children can develop a sense of belonging to and ownership of.

Whilst maths progression frameworks are handy for providing an indication of next steps in learning, one potential risk is that we focus on the narrow outcomes which are the tip of the iceberg and not the input necessary for conceptual understanding to develop, nor *how* to do this.

In order to support a developmentally appropriate interpretation of national expectations and research, we need to consider how young children learn. In Scotland, the national document *Realising the Ambition: Being Me*[4] is a useful starting point, particularly the sections on Playful Numeracy and Mathematical Development. Children learn through doing – exploring their environments physically – and through their social interactions with each other and adults around them, where the thinking and reasoning can be clarified and extended.

This is why my five Rs for developmentally appropriate mathematical education during the Early Level are:

- the Right to learn maths

- the Responsibilities of the practitioner

- the Routines we develop

- the Resources we employ

- Re-imagining the spaces in which children can play.

The Right to learn maths

When we consider why a child may need to know about and use maths, it can be helpful to think about the purpose of maths. Firstly, it is a tool that helps us do things and often more easily and efficiently. It's also a different perspective or lens that develops our understanding about how the world works. It is about reasoning and making sense of what is happening through looking for patterns and connections, similarities and differences. Across all societies, humans use maths in a variety of ways and cultural differences emerge which require recognition and appreciation.

Every child has a right to learn maths regardless of their developmental age or ability. The maths that happens must be relevant to a child's interests and needs. It has to make sense to a child and therefore needs to be part of their everyday lives at home and nursery or school. The 'targeted support' advocated by the EEF guidance can be achieved by practitioners recognising which children may need more time, or who may need assistance to make sense of the language of maths. The EEF guidance also emphasises the need to ensure that children who need support receive it from the most experienced staff who should access professional development, training and support for this role.

We need to build upon what children know and can do rather than trying to fill the gap between where they are at and what a curriculum target or benchmark is saying a child ought to be able to know and do at the end of Primary 1. This begins by observing our children playing. For example, a group of children enjoy being dogs. We can do a brief brainstorm with a colleague and ask ourselves 'Where's the maths in that?' as illustrated in Figure 1:

Figure 1: 'Where's the maths in being a dog?'

Initially it is common for educators to focus on subcategories such as 'time' or 'estimate'. This is why 'Tell me more. . .' is an important additional phrase. It helps the adults discuss the possibilities. Eventually, with practice, adults are able to think about maths challenges, investigations or problems that need to be solved in relation to the child's interest.

If this approach is refined and developed, then the results can be transformative for both parties. It is particularly powerful for children with additional support needs or a when a behaviour is perceived as a problem. In one nursery, a passion for digging that caused significant issues was channelled into mathematical discoveries around holes through asking 'Where's the maths in that?'

The Responsibility of the practitioner

As early years professionals, our job is to help our children develop a love of maths that enables them to thrive in our complex societies and value and care for this precious world in which we live. If we have had negative childhood experiences of maths, then this is a chance for us to re-write the script and ensure this does not happen to any child with whom we work.

The importance of investing in high quality professional development in early years maths cannot be emphasised enough in order to ensure developmentally appropriate maths is happening. More so, we need to be able to identify next steps in learning and ways of extending children's skills, knowledge and understanding. There are many organisations that provide free materials and guidance such as the National Centre for Excellence in the Teaching of Mathematics[5] that can be a useful starting point.

Children do not magically learn maths. They need support to do so from adults who:

■ Engage in mathematical conversations and take time to ensure that the vocabulary is explained and makes sense to children

■ Model mathematical mark-making and representations such as the use of charts and tables as part of their interactions with children

■ Encourage children to choose their own mathematical graphics and strive to elicit the mathematical meaning and reasoning behind these

■ Are able to make links between successful learning in maths, children's overall physical and emotional wellbeing and their cognitive development. The Building Blocks for Learning from Turnaround for Children provide helpful evidence and guidance to this effect[6]

■ Are able to make the most of outdoor as well as indoor opportunities for mathematical experiences.

The Routines we develop

As well as responding to children's needs, we can integrate the mathematics into our day in a focused and intentional way through embedding maths into the everyday routines. It can be helpful to compile a list of routines and then consider the maths that could happen. For example:

■ Self-registration upon arrival at your nursery

■ Washing hands

■ Getting changed in and out of outdoor clothing

■ Having snack

■ Visiting local greenspace

■ Tidying up

■ Gardening

■ Using the woodwork area

If we consider handwashing, we could:

■ Provide a series of photographs showing how to wash hands: 1st, 2nd, 3rd, etc.

■ Learn a song so we know we are washing our hands for the correct amount of time.

■ Provide a countdown clock or timer and show children how to use this.

■ Offer a choice of soap dispenser in different sized bottles and notice the volume of soap decreasing over several days.

■ Have some paper hand towels cut in half so that children can compare the size and learn about making the quantity of towels go further.

We can also make the most of gathering times when a group of children have come together and are ready for, and interested in, undertaking a shared event. Sometimes this can precede a key time of the day, such as when lunch is shared together. This could involve a short, playful activity such as a quick game, puzzle, number song, rhyme or story with a specific intentional focus. This is the element that can gradually be extended in Primary One and Two so that eventually children transition into a more formal approach. This is clearly illustrated in Anna Ephgrave's book *Year One in Action.*[7]

A useful website is Maths through Stories.[8] It has lots of suggestions that are linked to specific aspects of maths. Many of the books have an outdoor theme or focus which makes them suitable for reading outside.

The other key routine to develop is fun and friendly ways of supporting families to enjoy maths together. Suggestions such as baking, reading stories that reference maths concepts, sharing number rhymes and learning simple games to share help make connections between home and school.

The Resources we employ

Care is needed when it comes to acquiring maths resources. Both staff and children should understand their purpose. It is also important to consider that mathematical tools are needed in different areas of provision. For example, rulers and tape measures are needed in the woodwork and gardening area. Scales are useful for preparing snacks and in role play. Adults need to role model the use of maths tools and manipulatives so that children learn both how to use them and why they are necessary. Research by Jay and Betenson[9] suggests that even children as old as six and seven benefit from using their fingers as a maths tool. Fingers can be used for counting, gestures and displaying quantities of numbers in different ways. They help children express their understanding of maths concepts.

In addition to maths tools and manipulatives, we can apply the 'diversity principle' to much of our basic provision outside and in. It's a small change to resourcing that can make a significant difference. Acquiring real-life, natural and junk items that have no fixed purpose or defined use has a lot of mathematical value, especially if there is a diversity of offerings. For example, asking children and their families to donate a couple of clothes pegs will create an interesting collection for free. The pegs can be sorted in a variety of ways: size, colour, spring tension, mass, shape and material. As children look at, talk about and use the variety of pegs, the descriptions and discussions that happen will naturally use a greater variety of mathematical language than a pack of thirty pegs bought in a pack.

The impact within children's play is noticeable. The children learn that not all pegs are manufactured equally. Some will be easier to use than others owing to the design or the type and quality of the spring. Some will work well for hanging up their art displays but will be hopeless for den building. The collection means that children now have to investigate, problem-solve, make decisions, undergo trial and error in their play and learn more about the properties of a peg in relation to its intended purpose. This is real-life application of the mathematical attributes of a peg!

We need to observe how children choose to use and play with these resources in order to extend children's maths skills knowledge and understanding. Figure 2 shows an example by a practitioner around the use of a wheelbarrow

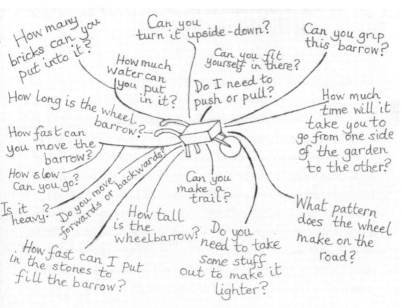

Figure 2: Supporting mathematical thinking when using a wheel barrow

Helping adults and children see the maths potential of everyday resources avoids the assumption that maths can only be taught through explicit foci using maths manipulatives Outside, the possibilities are further enhanced by the interactions that occur between a child, an object, the environment in which it is used in combination with the ever-changing multi-sensory nature of the weather and seasons. These variables and phenomena form an essential part of the Loose Parts Theory advocated by Simon Nicholson.[9]

Reflecting upon the mathematics of playing with an object can also be undertaken with children. One teacher noted that the go-kart tyres were very popular. She invited interested children to take them to the school playing field, where together they played with the tyres and discussed maths as they did so. This can be a valuable approach as part of assessing children's understanding of different maths concepts.

Re-imagining the spaces in which children can play

If you observe young children playing freely in an environment, their ability to navigate obstacles, lift, move and stack objects are all examples of geometric experiences that come naturally to them. Without the time to explore spaces and shapes in all their forms, it becomes harder for children to develop the intuition, imagination and spatial awareness needed to understand the key concepts which underpin this aspect of maths. Those children who struggle with number work often find they can identify with shape and spatial awareness. It is a form of mathematical thinking which involves feeling, moving and physically exploring with the whole body.

Derek Haylock and Anne Cockburn state the need for

educators to '*recognise the significance and value of informal and intuitive experience of shape and spatial concepts through play and other activities in and out of the classroom*'[10]. Thus we need to increase the mathematical possibilities of our outdoor and indoor environments through close attention to the layout and set up.

Children need to be able to see their space from different perspectives and to learn about space through moving in, out, up, down and around structures – vertically and horizontally. This involves thinking about the orientation of every feature as well as the space as a whole such as:

- A variety of levels: These include horizontal working surfaces at different heights, including below ground level, such as a sunken pit or a puddle

- Slopes: these help children to explore speed, distance and time through their own movement, use of wheeled toys and exploring how water flows or objects travel.

- Height: mounds, trees, small ladders, fixed playground equipment can all help children experience height. It may also help to build this into your off-site visits so that children can experience large-scale height and how small the world can seem from above.

- Opportunities to stretch and reach: this is estimation and checking in action. We could think about the placement of objects to this effect.

- Partitions and holes of different sizes and shapes, placed at different heights: this helps children develop spatial awareness and the need to move items to make them fit through spaces. A tunnel is one long hole to crawl through.

In addition, children need to:

- Discover a range of shapes and patterns that exist in different environments, especially being able to compare man-made and natural spaces and the patterns that shapes create.

- Investigate sand, snow, mud and clay to sculpt, manipulate and flatten shapes.

- Engage with mathematical environmental print and learn about its relevance and purpose.

- At a micro-level, the availability of blocks for construction and imaginative play support this aspect of maths.

Finally, by focusing on rights, responsibilities, routines, resources and re-imagining the spaces in which children can play, we can offer children the opportunity to learn maths in a child-centred way. This is not about reducing the rigour, but about adding depth and detail that provide more holistic and motivational ways of teaching maths in the early years. ☐

Acknowledgements: Thanks to Dr Helen Williams for being a critical friend and Madelaine Gattouchi for permission to use her illustration in Figure 2.

Chapter 11
Raising the status of the early years workforce and what this means for children's experience

Aline-Wendy Dunlop, Marion Burns and Lynn McNair

IN THIS CHAPTER we draw on the expertise of three differently experienced early childhood educators to consider three main issues affecting the status and continuous development of the early years workforce 0-8 in Scotland today. These are:

- What makes an effective educator?

- The power of study

- Practitioner enquiry.

In 2008 the Scottish government published the *Early Years Framework 0-8*. This influential document talked about a new level of ambition in early years, with transformational change, including this statement:

> Children and families are supported by a workforce which is highly skilled, well trained, appropriately rewarded, well supported, highly valued by all and with attractive career paths. . . Those who work with children and families in the early years are committed to their own continuous professional development to improve their knowledge and skills. Employers provide resources, advice and support to deliver this effectively. . . [1]

Scotland's education system is underpinned by a set of national objectives and core values that are aspirational, visionary, and resolute that every child has an entitlement to high quality educational provision leading to positive outcomes. Achieving these objectives will require a suitably qualified workforce where cohesion, collaboration and communication coalesce to form a highly effective system – a system that when carefully aligned, with the same goals in mind, can achieve great things.

In reality success boils down to how effectively in practice each educator employs their qualifications and skills. For the vast majority of educators, the initial qualification signals the start of their career journey. That career is increasingly influenced by internal and external pressures on the educator to continuously upskill, deepen and broaden their professional knowledge to ensure they develop the capacity to make a positive difference to the life chances of children.

It is therefore worth considering what it is it that sets *effective* educators apart: the attributes they possess are not finite and certainly not exclusive, though perhaps finely tuned through further study or practitioner enquiry.

Ways into the workforce. . . and ways forward

Traditionally, the career path of educators working in the Early Learning and Childcare (ELC) sector has varied. Unlike teachers in schools, they arrive at the workplace via vastly different starting points and qualification routes. The creation of the regulatory body, the Scottish Social Services Council (SSSC), in 2001 required the ELC workforce to be registered to work in the social services sector and to achieve a minimum level of qualification (SCQF Level 7 for ELC practitioners, and SCQF Level 9 for managers and lead practitioners).[2] On the other hand, teachers working with children between three- and eight-years old (and beyond) follow the initial teacher education route at SCQF Level 10 and are required to register with the General Teaching Council for Scotland (GTCS).[3/4]

Siraj and Kingston's 2015 review of the ELC sector and out of school care (OSC) sector in Scotland described a workforce that is diverse and disparate.[5] Most notably the review found a disparity between pay and conditions, recruitment arrangements and expectations around the workforce's initial qualifications. The authors made 31 recommendations which included the restructuring of all qualifications for the ELC workforce and for new and creative initial graduate degrees to be devised for educators leading learning in the ELC sector. They also recommended access to additional continuing professional learning opportunities, with many ELC educators stepping up to the challenge, achieving graduate level qualifications such as the BA Childhood Practice and Professional Development Awards.

Interestingly, the review drew comparisons with the initial training of teachers, who undertake a graduate level qualification followed by a period of probation before receiving full registration as a newly qualified teacher. Continuous lifelong professional learning (CLPL) for the teaching profession is a requirement born out of a long standing national agreement and mandated by the GTCS to maintain an exacting standard of professional competency.[6]

The SSSC's and the GTCS's focus on professionalism, where the individual is required to meet a set of nationally agreed core standards, complement the Scottish government's objective of further improving the quality and consistency of educational provision for all of Scotland's children and young people.

Regulatory and scrutiny bodies such as the Care Inspectorate and Education Scotland jointly evaluate the quality and effectiveness of nursery provision against a framework of care standards and quality indicators. Education Scotland evaluates the effectiveness of provision in schools. Inspection activity demonstrates that effectiveness does not equate purely with the existence of a battery of additional qualifications.

What makes an effective educator?

There is a balance to be struck when making a judgement about effectiveness and its impact on improving outcomes for children. When it comes down to determining the existence of high quality provision, the inspector looks in the round at qualifications, leadership, and length of experience as well as competency. There is a strong focus during inspection visits on how all of these elements contribute to the overall quality of provision: most notably the prevalence of effective interactions and relevant, meaningful play experiences made possible by educators who are attuned to the needs of the child. Similarly, educators who are creative with curriculum guidance, and time, in spaces that are inclusive, are noted to be motivating and enabling for children.

Effective educators are fleet of foot in busy playrooms and classrooms; they are responsive, reflexive and passionate about their pedagogy. They actually understand what the word 'pedagogy' means and enact it in their practice. Effective educators form teams that exhibit an open-minded, permissive, dynamic attitude to working with and for children. In effective settings, educators plan intentionally and responsively support opportunities for children to exploit the possibilities for learning that exist in inspiring spaces outdoors and indoors. Effective educators are advocates for children, empowering them to have agency over what and how they learn, at a pace which mirrors their curiosity and thirst for knowledge.[7]

Effective educators offer authentic choice; they listen and respond to children's voices rather than invite opinion but then follow their own adult agenda. Effective educators realise the power they hold. They reimagine the Early Level curriculum in ways that connect, build on and deepen children's knowledge. The effective educator thinks developmentally, taking sensitive account of the skills, capacities and dispositions children bring with them to the learning spaces. They maximise the potential children possess to solve problems, to explore and to make sense of their world. The effective educator embraces play as pedagogy.[7]

In recent years, Scotland has led the way in making Continuous Learning for Professional Leadership (CLPL) accessible and desirable for aspiring leaders of learning. Research confirms that strong leadership sits alongside high quality effective provision.[8] Iram Siraj asserts 'it is imperative that provision is of the highest possible impunity.'[9] A number of leadership reviews also stress the importance of questioning assumptions and of emphasising 'leadership and goals that address social injustices for children, families and the early childhood workforce.'[10]

We propose then that qualifications in themselves do not result in high quality experiences for children in early learning and childcare settings or in early primary. Rather the existence of the educator's strong professional identity and values must be evident in practice. Practice must be responsive, reflexive, rooted in a pedagogy of listening,[11] where the educator's interactions give voice to the child – **authentically**.

Effective educators – the power of study

Pedagogical practice must be instilled by love and passion, and effectively realised through a delicate balancing act of 'supporting, enriching and proposing on the one hand,'[12] while resisting imposed institutional structures, policy and traditions. Unfortunately, there are many traditions in the experiences of children 0-8 that differ culturally in what they value, what they measure and how they look and feel to the child. The importance of a shared vision and values cannot be underestimated.

Our shared experience of returners to study argues that this is a powerful way, both individually and collectively, to understand the effect on day-to-day practice of practitioners' values, knowledge, understanding and skills in working with children, families and teams. In Scotland the drive towards a fully qualified early years workforce must reach into primary school if the ambition of *Curriculum for Excellence* (*CfE*) is to be achieved.

What do we mean by this when it is obvious the early primary school workforce is qualified? We mean two things:

■ first that the workforce in ELC and in the early years of primary school should be equally recognised and recognisable, that they could be interchangeable

■ second, that the overlap in the age of nursery children and school entrants in any year is continuous, as should be the provision for them.

This leads naturally to what we read so clearly stated in the Ministerial Foreword to *Realising the Ambition*:

With the Early Level Curriculum for Excellence reaching to the end of primary 1, there also needs to be a consistency between practice in early learning and childcare and early primary school so that the transition is as seamless as possible. This refreshed national practice resource therefore speaks directly to and has been tested with primary school teachers as well as educators working in the early learning and childcare sector.[13]

Returning to study influences the professional identity of individuals. Study pathways can lead to a coming together of differently qualified practitioners in programmes which enhance mutual respect for varied contributions. We seek a blended early years and early primary workforce of lead practitioners in ELC (holding Scottish Level 9 or 10 qualifications), and GTCS registered teachers having an early years option in their initial degree. We also see the benefits of subsequently engaging in further study on postgraduate programmes together.[14/15]

Leadership in early childhood is exercised in many ways[16] and is understood to be complex and relational: it often involves an increased sense of personal agency, value and leadership dispositions, resulting in empowerment, effective practice, and shared and reflective pedagogical leadership throughout *CfE*'s Early Level.

The role of practitioner enquiry

However, study and qualifications are not the end of the effective practitioner story. Continuing a reflective and enquiring practice remains in the best interests of the child. Over the past decade much has been written about practitioner enquiry, which is defined as a 'finding out' or examination with a rationale and

137

methodology that can be elucidated or defended.[17] The results of practitioner enquiry can then be shared so it becomes more than reflection or personal enquiry.

We would argue that practitioner enquiry can dramatically change the lives of young children and early years practitioners, whilst simultaneously improving the Early Learning Childcare (ELC) setting, and indeed the early stages of primary education.[18] Research has the power to deepen thinking and understanding, and can radically and affirmatively influence transformational change in the early years context.

ELC is currently undergoing prodigious changes – for example the current Scottish government aims to fulfil its key election promise of almost doubling the entitlement of funded ELC for all three- and four -year-olds (and eligible two-year-olds). This has resulted in large public investments into workforce expansion and infrastructure.[19] As a spur, the expansion opens up opportunities for practitioner enquiry which may enable practitioners to articulate connections between pedagogy, principles and practice (and more) which have gone largely unexplored up until now.

Since practitioner enquiry adds to the intellectual climate of ELC and early primary settings, the expansion provides an opportunity for a wide range of scholarly forays into the early childhood domain. Never, then, has there been a better time for practitioners to practise their research skills, as children and adults venture into unknown territory.

Friedrich Froebel, a significant early years pioneer, argued that research must be rooted in the daily lives and experiences of children. The practitioners who work directly with children are, arguably, the best people to carry out research with them.[20]

They are the people who can share rich portrayals of the life of the setting and capture children's exhilarating, vivid life experiences. Their enquiries can take place in a variety of ways. It may be the research interest of one individual practitioner, or collectively when the whole team is interested in a particular issue/concern. Practitioner enquiry can reveal the interstices of everyday practice.

For example, Figure 1 illustrates how one practitioner, Vasinova·, ascribed a great deal of importance to the concept of the 'unique child.'[20] She followed one child as they moved through one Scottish ELC setting over a two-and-a-half-hour period. This ELC setting is based on Froebelian principles, one of his fundamental principles being that each child is a unique individual.

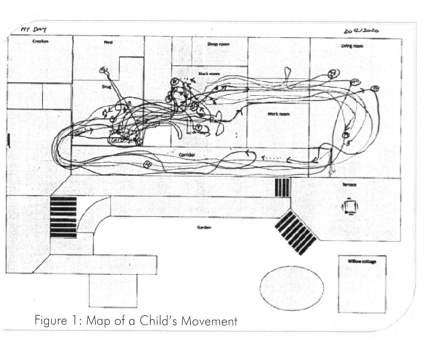

Figure 1: Map of a Child's Movement

Vasinova wrote up her research 'Follow me if you can'[21] with the intention of sharing it with other colleagues. She began with the following quote from Froebel's letters: 'In the interest of the children I have still another request to make – that you would record in writing the most important facts about each separate child.'[22] Froebel's concluded by saying: 'This research has confirmed how busy children can be in the ELC setting; it has also highlighted how much happens within short periods of time and how many stories the child has created. The hope is that this [research] will inspire all practitioners to step back, to 'see' the child in a way that respects their uniqueness. . .'

This practitioner-led research, then, proffers a new way of 'seeing'. Vasinova's careful articulation of the data was shared with colleagues, and several meetings took place where the team discussed the importance of the research. This resulted in the setting changing their practice – for example, a similar piece of work will be carried out with all children as they transition into the ELC setting, and at two other intervals throughout the year. This critical research could reveal what each child is interested in, or not, where they spend their time, who with and when and for how long. It is predicated on a model of practice that respects children's choice. The information could be vital to really understanding the uniqueness of each child and responding effectively.

Significantly, practitioner enquiry may also take place as full team research. For example, one Scottish ELC setting carried out a small action research project on the assessment and monitoring of young children. The practitioners strongly opposed the reductionist formal tick-box assessments produced by their doggedly parochial local authority and set about exploring other ways of capturing young children's learning.

This action research, conducted with children and adults, resulted in the ELC setting developing a new method to capture children's learning, which they named the 'Lived Story' approach. The 'Lived Story' is adapted from the canonical New Zealand work on Learning Stories. [23] The practitioners argued that the 'Lived Story' approach provided a method of seeing the complexities of children's experiences. This full team example demonstrated that practitioners do not need to simply accept top down directives, which continually converge around the topic of reductionist assessments, but can be creatively innovative in their work with young children.

Moving towards a coherent 'early level'

Inevitably in a time of change, some established practitioners may feel threatened or, in some ELC settings or P1 classrooms, there may be a complacent pedantry, with some practitioners keen to remain true to a *status quo* which signifies a somewhat empty conformity. Inherited conceptions may exist where some established practitioners express conceptual biases or hold on to over-simplified practices. They may therefore be sceptical of research that unearths more innovative ways of working with children.

With the publication of *Realising the Ambition*, these biases and practices must be questioned and overcome. Professional learning is a core aspect of the practitioner role and the days of remaining complacent have long passed.[24] Early years educators are carriers of cultural codes that shape children's experiences in the setting. As the above examples illuminated, practitioner enquiry can enable 'researchers' to explore the scholarly terrain and also question the dominant discourse and culture of their ELC setting.

As part of an early childhood postgraduate diploma programme some years ago, pairs of nursery and primary teachers studied together. They shared knowledge and planned for continuous experiences for children as they moved from nursery into primary school. Their existing nursery teacher assumed the job of Primary 1 teacher, while her study partner took up the nursery teacher role. After a year, the original P1 teacher moved on with the next group of nursery leavers to become their P1 teacher.

In this process, each pair of early years educators undertook work-based enquiry which covered curriculum, children as artists and designers, language and the young child, leadership, questioning pedagogy and a collaborating workforce – tasks in which they researched their own and their study partner's practices. In this unique collaboration between early childhood settings either side of school start, they realised a strong play-based transition to school, truly working as Early Level educators.

Conclusion

We believe that consideration of these three principal issues – defining what makes an effective educator; increasing common knowledge through study; and the ongoing reflective practices of an engaged workforce – will lead to a better understanding of what underpins career progression, the rising status of the early years workforce and the contradictions and dilemmas that remain today. There is continuing concern that despite the herculean efforts of the ELC workforce to do a great job for children and families, the status of early childhood 0-8 practice and its practitioners remains low across wider society. A raised status must be accompanied by raising the rewards. □

Chapter 12
What would a Scottish kindergarten stage look like?

Sue Palmer and Kate Johnston

THE EARLY LEVEL of Scotland's Curriculum for Excellence[1] begins when children are three years old and extends until the end of Primary 1 (P1), when most are aged six. The pedagogical practice recommended for Early Level is child-centred and play-based, which is the norm in nurseries. Unfortunately, when children transfer from nursery to school at age four or five it has usually meant a big change in the ethos of their education (see figure 1 on page 144).

It has therefore been heartening that, over the last few years, many P1 teachers have begun to introduce play-based pedagogy into their primary classrooms, often with support from local authority advisory services, as described in Chapter 6. The move has been accompanied by a groundswell of local and national training courses for P1 teachers (to make up for a sorry lack of attention to early child development in most initial teacher training courses) and some schools have employed nursery-trained staff to work alongside P1 teachers.

The publication of *Realising the Ambition: Being Me*[2] in 2020 should consolidate this welcome move in the direction of a Scottish 'kindergarten stage'. Indeed, less than a month after *Realising the Ambition* appeared, a 'blue skies thinking' report from Scotland's Futures Forum (*Schooling, Education and*

Kindergarten ethos	School ethos
Adults expected to support children at their individual developmental levels	Adults expected to teach children according to age-related standards
Emphasis on all-round development	Emphasis on literacy and numeracy
Outdoors (and in nature) as often as possible	Mainly indoors, often desk-based
Informal, flexible, child-led curriculum	Timetabled, subject-based curriculum
Children who are interested in reading/writing/numeracy supported at own level	Children expected to attain age-related targets in reading/writing/numeracy
Balance of self-directed play and adult-initiated activities	Activities mainly teacher-directed with little self-directed play

Figure 1: The ethos of education in kindergarten and school

Learning, 2030 and beyond)[3] envisioned that, by 2030, we'll have a kindergarten stage from three to eight. Certainly it's now reasonable to expect that, within a few years, the majority of Scottish P1 (and many P2) classes will adopt relationship-centred, play-based practice.

Unfortunately, however, Scotland's early school starting age means children still have to make the physical transition from nursery to school when they are four or five. This is a considerable social and emotional upheaval at that age. There's also the possibility that Scotland's cultural heritage (as described in Chapter 1) will prevent play-based pedagogy becoming fully embedded in P1 classrooms so that the change to developmentally appropriate education will be eroded over time, as is currently happening in England.[4]

Upstart therefore hopes that schools and nurseries soon start devising ways to educate and care for three- to six-year-olds together – on the same site – as a physical acknowledgement that this is a discrete developmental stage. In fact, as Chapter 9 illustrates, there have already been moves in this direction in some outdoor nurseries, and we at Upstart were expecting to see more innovations of this kind during 2020-21.

Sadly, the COVID-19 crisis has put paid to significant innovation for the time being. So, to give an idea of what we hope and expect, here are three likely imaginary scenarios, illustrating the next stage in Scotland's journey to 'a Nordic style kindergarten stage'.

The Lileen Hardy Primary School

This is a huge Victorian building in a major Scottish city, with a yearly intake of two P1 classes and a large nursery on site. Ms McMillan, the deputy head, has a Masters degree in Early Years so her remit is supervision of the nursery and P1 to P3.

Under Ms McMillan's supervision, the nursery and P1 classrooms have been located together in one wing of the school, the Early Level staff have collaborated for several years and P1 at Lileen's is now well-known for its play-based practice. Aided by a dedicated band of parent helpers (who love the new way of doing things), they've transformed a large open space outside their classrooms into a vibrant outdoor area for exploration and play-based learning.

The expansion of funded nursery hours in 2020 means many nursery children are in school for the same hours as P1 so, inspired by *Realising the Ambition,* Lileen's senior management team decided to create an Early Level Village (ELV), consisting of two vertically-grouped cohorts of three- to six-year-olds. Everyone could see the advantages of mixing the age-groups at this developmental stage, with the younger children learning from their older classmates, and the older children helping the little ones. Once the new intake was settled in, the groupings became more fluid – so that ELV indeed operates like a sort of village – a village that is raising eighty children.

The school also has access to a 'forest school area', a short minibus drive away. All Lileen Hardy staff receive basic training in outdoor education, appropriate to the age-range they teach (which in the case of Early Level is forest kindergarten training). ELV has been allocated a two-hour slot 'in the woods' every day so the 'elves' (as the children are now inevitably known) have plenty of access to nature, as well as free-flow access to their on-site outdoor area.

This year there are also two support assistants (for children with additional needs) in the Early Level at Lileen's, as well as at least one ELC student and several parent-helpers around. So every child in Ms McMillan's ELV has a named key worker and a great many other caring adults keeping an eye on their progress.

Parents and children are all delighted with the new arrangement. The P1 teachers are thrilled to be released from curriculum constraints so they can develop their observational skills and support the children in creating their own educational challenges. They also have time to engage with children in 'sustained shared thinking'[5] and to use learning journals, developmental observation charts and floor books for record-keeping and assessment. According to a PhD student who is monitoring 'The Lileen Hardy Experiment' for her PhD, the elves' progress so far is extremely gratifying.

Children's Garden Nursery

Children's Garden is a local authority nursery in a large post-industrial town which is officially designated an 'area of disadvantage'. The nursery has access to some local woodland space and, over the last few years, many of its practitioners have gained forest kindergarten qualifications. The children love spending time 'in the woods' and local parents and the community have supported the nursery's outdoor activities, building a storage shed, a yurt, a fire-pit and even a compost toilet. Enthusiasm among staff, parents and children for these woodland activities has been even keener since the COVID crisis.

The local authority is highly supportive of play-based learning at Early Level so, when Mrs Frederick, head teacher of Children's Garden, suggested expanding her nursery upwards into P1, they were sympathetic. However, they gently pointed out that she didn't have enough space and they couldn't afford to build an extension. Mrs Frederick then told them of a project in several Edinburgh nurseries, where children spend half the day outdoors in a 'forest nursery' environment and half indoors in a traditional nursery setting. Not only is it good for the children to spend half their time outdoors, it also means that each nursery building can cater for twice as many bodies.

The local authority was immediately interested, especially as they knew that the next year's P1 class in the main primary school fed by Children's Garden was worryingly oversubscribed. They therefore brokered an arrangement for the school to swap one of its teachers for one of Children's Garden's early years practitioners, meaning that Children's Garden could now accept P1 children, while the primary school had an early years practitioner (EYP) to help develop play-based practice in P1.

Aided by excellent online mentoring from Edinburgh, Children's Garden created Scotland's first state-funded outdoor kindergarten for children (Woodland Weans Kindergarten), much to the delight of local parents who soon saw the positive impact on children under seven of learning and playing outdoors in nature, rather than traditional schooling. Indeed, the entire local community, inspired by Children's Garden's pioneering spirit, has rallied to support them with fundraising activities. The first of these equipped every child with warm, waterproof outdoor gear. The second opened up new horizons by turning an empty retail unit close by the nursery into a 'design studio' (Mrs Frederick calls it the 'Malaguzzi-style atelier') for an on-site artist who works with the children and parents for a percentage of the year.

This enthusiastic community support of the Woodland Weans Kindergarten has generated a great deal of publicity – not just in Scotland but worldwide. And the town's reputation as community-led trailblazers has already attracted a couple of new businesses to the area.

Taigh na Cloinne Village School

Taigh na Cloinne Village School is a rural school with three full-time teachers, including the head, Mr Geddes, who is very keen on education for sustainability and has always made full use of the school grounds and surrounding countryside in implementing *Curriculum for Excellence*.

The school also houses a nursery class run by Ms Owen, a senior early years practitioner, who has alerted Mr Geddes to the importance of play in developing the self-regulation skills, creativity and intrinsic motivation to learn that will benefit children throughout their education. She has also pointed out that self-directed play lays the foundations for skills they'll need in future employment, as foreseen by the World Economic Forum.

Trading, 2022
Analytical thinking and motivation
Active learning and learning strategies
Creativity, originality and initiative
Technology design and programming
Critical thinking and analysis
Complex problem-solving
Leadership and social influence
Emotional intelligence
Resoning, problem-solving and ideation
Systems analysis and evaluation

Figure 2: World Economic Forum: The Future of Jobs Report[6]

Not surprisingly, therefore, Taigh na Cloinne Village School has embraced *Realising the Ambition* with open arms. Ms Owen is now head of Early Level and – ably supported by the former 'infant teacher' – provides play-based education and care for children up to the end of P2. (The 'middle class' consists of P3 to P5 and Mr Geddes teaches P6/7).

All the classes make use of the wonderful outdoor environment and opportunities for involvement with the community. The Early Level children spend at least half their time learning outdoors and have forged strong links with local 'grannies' and 'grandpas', who last year helped them plan and plant a kitchen garden (including polytunnel), so they can grow, prepare and eat healthy food all year round.

The school has even had two articles in the *Times Educational Supplement*: one by Mr Geddes on the use of the outdoor environment to stimulate children's interest in STEM subjects, sustainability and critical thinking (which mentions the Early Level healthy food project); and one by Ms Owen ('Getting the Four Capacities Right from The Start') on how the under-sevens of Taigh na Cloinne Village School are now involved in planning for their own learning, the development of the school environment and ways of engaging with the community.

Barriers to implementing a kindergarten stage

Back in real life, it isn't such plain sailing, of course. Some schools and settings will be put off experimenting with Early Level reorganisation because of logistical and regulatory issues, such as adult:child ratios and staff qualifications. The growing professionalism of early years practitioners (including their understanding of child development and play-based learning) is not yet recognised by many members of the educational establishment. But Scotland's ambitions for the Early Level will not be realised until we have achieved a genuinely 'blended workforce', where the qualifications of early years professionals are valued as highly as those of primary teachers. We hope Chapter 11 of this book will be helpful in this respect.

There may also be problems regarding inspection. Since nurseries are currently inspected by the Care Inspectorate and schools by Education Scotland, there would probably have to be some degree of regulatory reform. However, special provision is already made for the inspection of kindergarten classes in Montessori and Steiner schools so it shouldn't be too difficult to extend this to 'straight-through Early Level' classes in other nurseries and schools.

Another likely barrier to success is the continued existence of the P1 SNSA (Scottish National Standardised Assessments in literacy and numeracy) and its related (highly unrealistic) benchmarks. As long as national and local government officials insist on assessing the literacy and numeracy skills of four- and five-year-olds, many P1 teachers will feel obliged to teach in the old-fashioned way. We need national recognition that age-related educational 'standards' are not developmentally appropriate during early childhood (i.e. before the age of eight).

Perhaps, if enough politicians read Part Three of this book, they will soon abandon literacy and numeracy testing at P1 and introduce the EDI (the highly regarded Early Development Instrument, used with this age group in Canada and Australia). In the meantime, to maintain the integrity of play-based pedagogy, we hope P1 teachers and their managers will simply act as if the P1 SNSA doesn't exist (except for the miserable couple of days on which it has to be administered). We also urge head teachers to support parents who wish to opt their children out of the P1 SNSA.

There will, of course, be further barriers to implementing an effective kindergarten stage, particular to individual schools and settings. For instance, many Scottish primary schools have difficulty providing all-day access to outdoor areas and natural environments. Solving these specific difficulties will require open-mindedness, curiosity, creative thinking and willingness to collaborate on behalf of schools' senior management and local authority personnel. If this is forthcoming, we reckon most problems can be solved through consultation between early years educators, parents and community activists – people who know the buildings, neighbourhood and children concerned. As Children's Garden Nursery and Taigh na Cloinne Village School suggest, the development'of Early Level outdoor facilities can be an excellent focus for community engagement.

Advantages of implementing a kindergarten stage
There are so many advantages to the innovations we're suggesting that it's difficult to list them all. So let's just take for granted the arguments throughout this book in favour of adopting *Realising the Ambition* practice guidance for all under-sevens, as a way of helping all children fulfil their educational potential, while improving their health and well-being – and thus, in the long term, the social and economic well-being of the nation as a whole.

But there are also obvious benefits for children, parents and teachers/EYPs in abandoning the highly disruptive physical transition from nursery to school the year children turn five. There is no good argument for this highly significant (and sometimes traumatic) 'transition' at such a formative stage in children's development – transition in the year they turn six or seven (as in most countries of the world) makes much more sense. If all Scottish schools/settings could find ways to introduce a 'straight-through Early Level' there would be no need for a

Give Them Time campaign, nor for the wasteful expenditure of time and money when local authorities battle to send children to school against their parents' wishes (see Chapter 8).

As illustrated in the examples above, establishing a 'straight-through Early Level' immediately raises local awareness of the importance of early childhood education and care. A national change to this system would provide a platform for explaining the significance of child development to the entire Scottish public and thus help destroy the damaging misconceptions about play identified by Suzanne Zeedyk in Chapter 1. That would sit very comfortably alongside our present government's commitment to 'Getting It Right for Every Child' and making Scotland 'the best place in the world to grow up'.

A 'straight-through Early Level' would also benefit everyone working in early childhood education and care because – as a ring-fenced stage in our education system, covering three to four years of children's lives – it would raise the status of early childhood education and care. It would also create what the authors of Chapter 11 call a 'blended workforce', thus shining a light on the particular skills of early years practitioners, which would hopefully lead to increased remuneration for this seriously underpaid section of the workforce. The longer time frame also offers improved opportunities for career progression. And it should guarantee that anyone working with the under-sevens (including primary-trained teachers) would receive training in child development, play-based pedagogy and outdoor education and care.

From a long-term educational perspective, there's another big advantage to a 'straight-through Early Level'. When children spend three to four years in the same setting – with no disruptive transition at age four or five – there is time for observation, identification of problems and the provision of early therapeutic support. Chapter 9 describes how Finnish EY practitioners identify many additional support needs during the kindergarten stage. Then, working with parents and specialist therapists, they offer targeted support as early as possible, so that developmental problems are ameliorated or (sometimes) even solved before children start school. Indeed, for many the simple 'Gift of Time'[7] would mean that additional support needs never develop.

Back to the future

Many of the advantages of what Upstart calls 'a Nordic-style kindergarten stage' relate to the biological needs of children during this extremely formative stage of their lives. As pointed out in Chapter 2, the centrality of outdoor play and learning to a kindergarten ethos contributes to children's all-round development and long-term physical and mental health. Outdoor play has been the birth-right of children throughout the millennia and research by evolutionary biologists[8] shows how greatly it has contributed to the survival of our species. For the long-term well-being of children and society, the decline of outdoor play must be reversed and, as the American Academy of Paediatrics explains, the best place to reverse it is during early childhood.[9]

The mixed-age 'vertical grouping' adopted in all three of our kindergarten scenarios is another advantage from the perspective of evolutionary biology. Since time immemorial, young children's emotional and social development has been advanced, not only by their interactions with caring adults, but through play (especially outdoor play) with other children.

Three-year-olds have always learned by watching older friends and siblings, and six- and seven-year-olds have always grown in confidence and competence by helping and taking responsibility for the little ones. As Sarah Latto illustrated in Chapter 7, adults are often unaware of this eternal truth but children, given half a chance, will remind them.

And, finally, it takes a village to raise a child. As all our scenarios show, a kindergarten stage is the 21st century version of the proverbial child-rearing village. Nowadays, professionals care for children while parents are at work but every community still feels its inevitable responsibility to the next generation. In our experience, parents, grandparents and other adults in the local area are usually eager to help improve facilities for this age-group, and give local young children 'a good childhood'. The establishment of a kindergarten stage provides the perfect focus for community involvement and regeneration.

Realising the Ambition: Being Me has provided Scotland with a magnificent opportunity to inform, educate and enthuse the nation on behalf of the next generation. We hope and pray Scotland will take it. □

SECTION THREE

The wider context

Since child development is a bottom-up process, this book can't ignore what happens before the age of three. To put Upstart's vision into a wider context, here are two more perspectives, this time focusing on the very early years.

- ■ John Frank, Professor of Public Health, and Dr Rosemary Geddes provide a public health perspective on child development and describe how, thanks to the cultural assumptions described in Chapter 1, the Scottish government missed a golden opportunity to narrow the poverty-related attainment gap.

- ■ Alan Sinclair, founder and Chief Executive of the Wise Group, a social enterprise, spent seventeen years 'hauling long-term unemployed young people off the dole'. Here he explains – from a long-term social and economic perspective – why Scotland needs to address the attainment gap from the earliest possible moment.

Many chapters in the previous two sections have argued that a relationship-centred, play-based kindergarten stage will be beneficial to all children, but particularly those from disadvantaged homes. In the long term, setting up such a kindergarten stage means a legal adjustment to Scotland's system of universal state services, since – to preserve its integrity – it must be recognised as a separate entity from the schooling system.

But it's also clear that Scotland needs to provide targeted support for those children whose development goes seriously off-track before the age of three. We need to identify where and why this is happening and provide appropriate support from the very start – indeed even before children are born.

Our current system of universal services was established over seventy years ago, after the Second World War. Children's lives and lifestyles have changed immensely since then, and it's likely that there will be even more radical changes in the wake of the COVID pandemic and Brexit, not to mention the ongoing challenges of climate change. Now that neuroscience has alerted us to the huge significance of early childhood experiences to long-term health and well-being, an *ad hoc,* lip-service approach to the early years sector is no longer sustainable.

It's time to recognise early years as the essential foundation upon which Scotland's success depends – not only in terms of education, but of health, well-being, social stability and economic success. It's time to get early years policy right from the start.

Chapter 13
A public health perspective on child development – and on Scotland's approach to assessment at P1

Prof John Frank and Dr Rosemary Geddes

THROUGHOUT the world of professional and academic public health, the 2008 Report of the WHO Commission on the Social Determinants of Health, chaired by Sir Michael Marmot[1], was a fundamental game-changer. That ground-breaking report has been invaluable for promoting sound, evidence-based child development policies to globally improve population health and function over the entire life-course.

Less well known is a preliminary in-depth report by one of the many 'knowledge networks' for that Commission, focused on Early Child Development (ECD) and led by Professor Clyde Hertzman at the University of British Columbia. In that sub-section of the full WHO Report, the following central principle is supported by extensive citations of high-quality studies on this topic, going back many decades:

> A significant outcome of this knowledge synthesis was
> the creation of a framework (see Figure 1) based on
> Bronfenbrenner's (1986) model that identifies and
> characterizes the environments that play a significant

The chapter is dedicated to the lead author's strong memories of his brilliant colleague Professor Clyde Hertzman (who died suddenly and prematurely in 2013).

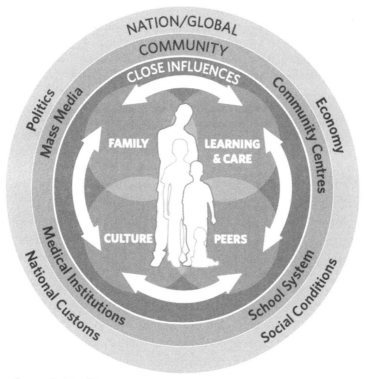

Figure 1: Total Assessment Model for Early Child Development[3]

role in setting the nurturant conditions experienced
by children globally. A variation on the original model
of Urie Bronfenbrenner, the framework acts as a
guide to understanding the relationships between
these environments, putting the child at the centre of
her or his surroundings.

The environments are not strictly hierarchical, but are
overlapping and interconnected. At the most intimate
level is the family environment. At the next level are
residential communities (such as neighbourhoods),
relational communities (such as those based on
religious or other social bonds), and the ECD service

environment. Each of these environments (where the child grows up, lives, and learns) is situated in a broader socioeconomic context that is shaped by factors at the regional, national, and global level. The framework affirms the importance of a life-course perspective in decision making regarding ECD. Actions taken at any of these environmental levels will affect children not only in present day, but also throughout their lives.[2]

In their comprehensive review of the scientific evidence about childhood determinants of lifelong health and function, the authors point out the especially critical role of Early Child Development programmes, in which they include all pre-school learning in organised educational environments, from nursery through to the end of kindergarten.

They point out that the most influential aspects of those childhood experiences are not only language-cognitive inputs – such as 'three Rs' content'– but importantly also aspects of social-emotional and physical development. This includes the relationships children learn to develop and nurture with others (both teachers and fellow pupils), the socialisation required to be a functioning member of a classroom, and *play:*

'Young children need to spend their time in warm responsive environments that protect them from inappropriate disapproval and punishment. They need opportunities to explore their world, to play, and to learn how to speak and listen to others.'[4]'

This chapter aims to explain and discuss, in the Scottish policy context, one of the most important ways that a high-functioning public health system should facilitate and support such high-quality ECD. This should involve regular and consistent monitoring of holistic measures of child development at the population level, combined with repeated feedback of those results to policy makers, programme leads, and the teaching/administrative staff of early years education as well as their parent communities.

The history of and rationale for the Early Development Instrument

First, we shall briefly recap the importance of ECD programmes for optimising the development of each entire birth cohort, to enable their attainment of their full human potential over the life course. On this, there is near-universal scientific agreement that:

- Neurodevelopmental research confirms that the brain is most malleable in the very early years when windows of opportunity exist for the optimal development of different skills.[5]

- Both public health professionals and economists now argue that investing in the early years is not only necessary to tackle inequalities in later health and well-being; it is moreover the most lucrative investment a country can make.[6]

- Monetary returns to a society over the life span of an individual are expected to more than repay the initial investment.[7]

It follows that ECD programmes aiming to help all children achieve their full potential require some reliable measure of their success, in terms of sequential, standardised assessments made, over many years, of a broad spectrum of child development indicators, in representative samples of entire birth cohorts born into each society. Only by providing the ECD programme providers and decision-makers with such 'end-point' data can they adjust their programmes to improve them.

Several countries have fully incorporated this principle into their national measurement programmes for children's health and development. For example, Australia's national government has paid for the administration and analysis of a P1-teacher-completed form – the Australian-adapted version of the Early Development Instrument (EDI) – for over 90 per cent of their P1 students' developmental milestones (appropriate for age 5-6) every three years for over a decade.[8]

And Canada, despite its strongly devolved system of education across ten provinces and three territories, has gradually increased the coverage, with this same assessment tool, of their P1 ('first-grade' – age 5-6) students over the last decade. Yet the UK and especially Scotland lag behind, with no current plans to do such holistic testing of P1 students' developmental milestones. This policy impasse persists despite considerable evidence – reviewed below – that this would be feasible, popular with stakeholders, and useful for decision-makers and educational professionals. This chapter will explore some of the possible reasons for the impasse – but first we need to briefly review the history of and rationale for the EDI.

The creator of the Early Development Instrument

The original creator of the EDI was a charismatic child psychiatrist and human-development researcher, Dr Dan Offord of McMaster University in Hamilton, Ontario, Canada. He was not only scientifically brilliant, but also a man of immense generosity and warmth. For example, even though his heavy clinical caseload always included many troubling complex cases which would exhaust many clinicians, he chose to set up, find funding for, administer and personally attend an annual summer camp in the Canadian woods for 'disturbed children'.

By the 1990s, Offord had read everything already published in the field of measuring human development in early childhood, spanning multiple professional and scientific disciplines. He quickly saw that most of the then widely-used instruments for assessing how a child was developing at, say, school entry (P1 in Scotland), were completely impractical for use with an entire national birth cohort.

That is because they require highly skilled direct observation of child's behaviour, and/or expensive, labour-intensive, and onerous formal psychometric testing. He set out to create, from the best of many research-assessment protocols for ECD, a questionnaire that any P1 teacher could complete on each of their students in about 20-30 minutes, a few months after the start of P1 classes, when the teacher's knowledge of the students is well established.

Why test at P1 level (age five)?

Offord, extensively trained as an epidemiologist, realised that – in the Canadian early years educational environment of the 1990s, and still today in many jurisdictions – there was no universal provision of accessible and affordable early years care and education. Thus it was – and still is in many countries – not possible to ensure that a very large proportion of all children born in a given year (a 'birth cohort') would be collected in each community, in a setting where a standardised assessment of their developmental milestones could be accomplished – not possible, that is, until P1.

Moreover, Offord saw that it would never be practical to expect any level of government to pay the high costs for trained child development professionals (e.g. psychologists) to perform such assessments on all P1 students, at least every few years, in order to provide whole-population-level data on a birth cohort's developmental status at about the time of school entry.

Finally, Offord had the prescient insight that – in high-income countries – extensive measures were already being taken regularly *after* school entry, of children's educational attainment, typically through standardised assessments of students' arithmetical, literacy and general knowledge skills. He realised that it might therefore be acceptable to conduct a comprehensive assessment of each P1 student's broader developmental milestones – in terms of their skills in the physical, social, emotional, language, and self-governance domains of development, as seen in everyday life. These everyday indicators of child development are NOT at all similar to children's ability to score highly on arithmetical or language quizzes, which (as we will see below) are now universal in Scotland's P1 classrooms.

Importantly, these 'everyday' developmental milestones provide a valid and internationally comparable community-level indicator of just how well the entire first half-decade of each birth cohort's lives has prepared them for success in P1, and thus in school more generally. These data can then be fed back directly to local pre-school and kindergarten staff and administration, to help improve those programmes.

The progress of the EDI

Critically for policy impact within the typically short time horizon of modern democratically elected governments, such improvements would be demonstrable within just one or two years, by repeat EDI measurements in later birth cohorts. In short, Offord set out to create a simple questionnaire that validly assesses the

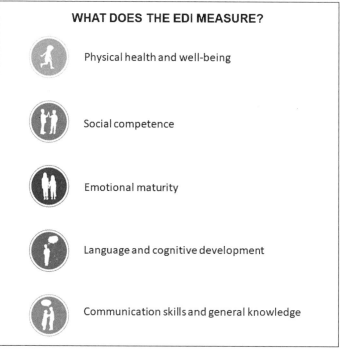

Figure 2: What does the EDI measure?

overall key developmental milestones of P1 students, through completion of a 104-question form by each child's P1 teacher (without any additional training), a few months after children start school.

By the end of the 1990s, he had created the EDI, extensively tested its internal consistency, various types of validity, repeatability, and acceptability to the teachers and other stakeholders, and piloted its use in selected Canadian schools – to much acclaim in the peer-reviewed literature.[9]

There then followed a challenging period of efforts to implement the EDI's use more widely in Canada, made difficult by the balkanisation of that country into 13 provinces and territories – all of them completely in charge of their own separate education systems. By 2009, a province-wide programme of repeat EDI measurements had been established only in the schools of British Columbia, set up and operated for many years by Professor Clyde Hertzman, whose work for the WHO Report is described above.[10]

It was in Australia, however, that the EDI (later slightly adapted to create Australian Early Development Census – the AEDC) became routinely applied to virtually every P1 student in the entire country as of 2009, through national – 'Commonwealth' – level legislation and funding. That funding was critical, because Australian states and territories have, as do Canadian provinces, authority over all aspects of education.

This was a bold move by Australia, and has today led to the development of the most comprehensive, high-quality body of scientific studies, including stakeholder evaluations, of how the EDI works, and how repeat waves of EDI results can be easily interpreted by local professionals and communities to improve their own pre-school programming.

Led by Prof Sally Brinkman at the University of Adelaide, the AEDC national measurement, analysis, and dissemination team has completed their fourth wave of measurement in virtually all the nation's far-flung P1 classrooms. Furthermore, the team has been sending those results back to each community, in formats suitable for parents, teachers and local officials to understand, and use in local decision-making.[11] While many other countries are currently developing such EDI-based national 'surveillance' systems for school-entry children's development, no other has progressed consistently as far and as fast as Australia.

The EDI in Scotland
– the East Lothian Pilot Study (2011-2)

In 2009, the senior author of this chapter (John Frank) had just established the Scottish Collaboration for Public Health Research and Policy (www.scphrp.ac.uk). Its mandate was to do useful research for Scottish public health decision-making, and one of our first four post-docs, Dr Rosemary Geddes, selected as her 'Early Life' project a pilot study of the EDI in Scotland – where neither it nor any comparable measure of early child development was in general use, although many schools were using various commercially-sold tests for assessing educational attainment of the 3Rs variety, at various ages, including P1.

In our 2011-12 pilot study dozens of very keen East Lothian P1 teachers completed the Scottish EDI (SEDI) for nearly 1100 students. Creating the SEDI involved only very minor adaptations of wording from the original Canadian English, which we accomplished in a pre-pilot of just a few dozen students and their teachers. The main pilot's results are well described in our peer-reviewed journal publication[12]. To quote its abstract:

Results suggested that the SEDI displayed adequate psychometric and discriminatory properties and is appropriate for use across Scotland without any further modifications. Children in the lowest socioeconomic status quintiles were 2-3 times more likely than children in the most affluent quintile to score low in at least one developmental domain. Even in the most affluent quintile though, 17% of children were 'developmentally vulnerable', suggesting that those in need cannot be identified by socioeconomic status alone. The SEDI offers a feasible means of providing communities with a holistic overview of school readiness for targeting early years interventions.

In the ensuing period, the project stakeholders in the East Lothian Council's educational and early-childhood departments waxed very enthusiastic about the EDI. They found it easy to communicate the results, using simple colour-coded bar graphs and maps supplied by our research team, to parent-teacher meetings in the six school catchment areas of the local authority.

How EDI results were applied in East Lothian – and what it cost

A subsequent unpublished study undertaken by a Masters student confirmed that many communities in East Lothian implemented programmes to address areas where the EDI indicated that the children were not performing well.[13] For instance, in the North Berwick cluster, 'Raising Children with Confidence' was a programme initiated to train teachers and support parents to improve children's resilience and self-confidence, and six 'Support from the Start' groups were set up in other clusters to engage with local parents, services and the wider community in improving outcomes for children during their early years. At local meetings of stakeholders and decision-makers, many reported finding the results *useful* – both for informing them about the most recent P1 birth cohort's developmental strengths and weaknesses, as well as for planning improvements in pre-school programming to address specific deficiencies documented by the EDI.

Finally, as perhaps the strongest indicator of local stake-holders' enthusiasm for the EDI, they raised the funds themselves in East Lothian to carry out a repeat-wave EDI measurement for all P1 students, a few years later. We were advisors on that project; however, we were unable to help the stakeholders move its analysis towards peer-reviewed publication due to resource constraints.

We computed the cost for each wave of EDI use as about £20 per P1 student tested, virtually all of which was used to cover the costs of substitute P1 teachers, during the approximately one day required for each of the regular teachers to complete the average two dozen students' EDIs for their class. Factoring in the added efficiencies of computer-entry of the EDI responses directly onto a secure internet site, there are very few other costs beyond substitute teacher wages. Since such waves are recommended only about every three years in Australia – the country with the most EDI experience – one can readily see that an annualised cost of less than £7 per student is relatively affordable for any high-income country.

In a nutshell, then, the EDI was clearly able to:

■   describe in detail the developmental status of a whole local authority's P1 birth cohort, at minimal cost and disruption (e.g. no direct student testing, which is known to be distressing for some at this age)

■   provide results that can be compared with other areas of Scotland, or indeed, other countries

■   provide scientifically validated local guidance, right down to the level of school clusters, to improve pre-school programming for birth cohorts coming along in the next few years.

Remarkably, the overall average percentage of children who were 'developmentally vulnerable' in all of East Lothian that year was 27 per cent – almost identical to that figure for British Columbia and Australia. [Of course, one must consider that East Lothian is far from the most deprived LA in Scotland; results from a pilot in the poorer parts of Glasgow, for example, would be quite different.]

What happened next: A tale of failed policy influence

As our small team of researchers and East Lothian partners sought then to report our very promising project results to Scottish Government's Education and Early Years departmental officials, a strange thing happened. Despite prompt publication of a full report in a respected academic journal and robust peer-review, we could not interest any officials, at the national Scottish level, in even hearing about the project *in camera*.

We had already foreseen that there might be legitimate concerns about using the EDI more widely in Scotland, rather than the traditional approach of assuming that every P1 child in every local authority had the same developmental needs and status, and then granting each local authority the same pre-school and primary-educational budget per capita (student) enrolled.

We foresaw that there might be problems in our implicitly suggesting – using EDI results – that pre-school and kindergarten resources should be allocated to each of Scotland's 32 local authorities in a way that was appropriate to their needs (but far more complicated). It might lead to demands from local authorities with lower EDI scores for extra resources to meet their greater needs. That in turn could lead to rancour between the main regions of Scotland, since a major predictor of EDI scores was, predictably, the Index of Multiple Deprivation of the residential households of the students.

But, in retrospect, we now believe that concern did not arise, because other considerations precluded the Education/Early Years officials of the time from even considering the use of a new measurement instrument for P1 students' developmental status, as a data platform for policy decision making.

In hindsight, the Scottish authorities were, by 2013-14, already planning (and thoroughly committed to) the launch, just a few years later, of a polar-opposite testing programme for P1 students. Those tests, now implemented over the last few years, despite extensive opposition in both community settings and the Scottish Parliament, involve what are essentially tablet-based educational attainment tests spanning the three Rs – but making no use of the P1 teachers' extensive knowledge of each student's more holistic developmental status.

Yet the scientific literature argues strongly that the latter indicators, based on what the child can do 'in everyday life', are much more powerful predictors of both later school and career success, than three Rs test results at age 5-6. In fact, many experts in ECD (some of them contributors to this book) hold the view that three Rs-based attainment testing in P1, so soon after curriculum-based teaching starts for the first time in most children's lives, merely accentuates the pre-existing differences between children from high-income and low-income families.

More educated and privileged families have often effectively coached their children in three Rs skills from a very early age, while the children of less educated, more deprived families –

who typically do not regard such coaching of toddlers as a cultural norm – have not. Nor in many cases do they necessarily have the ability to do so without extensive support from their local nursery.

Conclusions

Whatever the reasons, Scotland is now firmly on a trajectory of implementing *only* three Rs-based educational testing in primary schools, likely leading to pernicious longer-term effects, far beyond nursery and P1 settings. Public health experts, such as the authors, are particularly concerned about the potential for such a policy to increase the already very steep inequalities in lifelong health and productivity by social class in Scotland – some of the steepest in all of Europe, and generally unchanged in recent decades.[14]

That consequence is credible because three Rs-based testing, so early in childhood, will miss the key developmental delays of more disadvantaged children – many of them more basic in nature, such as anti-social behaviour, poor emotional control, excessive shyness and lack of 'executive functions' like forward planning and deferred gratification. The latter skills are now thought to be perhaps the most critical functions that children need to develop if they are to succeed, in both school writ large, and life.[15]

Sadly, such basic developmental delays can only be effectively addressed by appropriate early years teaching and parental support, so that these disadvantaged children are truly ready to succeed in primary school and beyond. Focusing on educational attainment at age 5-6 distracts from timely ECD interventions in earlier childhood to 'level the developmental playing field' across socio-economic levels in any society. Because of the neurobiology of human development, many of these more fundamental developmental deficits at age 5-6 can only be effectively prevented by strengthening ECD programmes targeted at much younger children, in order to have the biggest impact.

As noted by Professor Clyde Hertzman, 'inequity at the start (should be seen) as a violation of human rights' [16] as enshrined in the United Nations Convention on the Rights of the Child (UNCRC) [17] of which the UK is a signatory. The appended General Comment 7 of the UNCRC focuses exclusively on children 0-8 years, making explicit young children's right to enjoy their childhood to the full; the right to good health, learning, and playing.[18] Strengthening ECD programmes targeted to young children, based on regular, holistic developmental assessment with the EDI or a similar instrument, has the potential to not only improve the overall health, function and productivity of future generations in Scotland and more widely, but also reduce Scotland's stubbornly persistent inequities and health inequalities by social class. □

Chapter 14
Three Ps before three Rs:
child development before the Early Level

Alan Sinclair

READING, 'Riting and 'Rithmetic – the three Rs – are seen as the bedrock, the starting point of education and the benefits that flow. That is a great pity because this belief involves another R: Rubbish. What really come first are three Ps: Pre-conception, Pregnancy and Parents. When the 3Ps are in place, the 3Rs stop being Rubbish and children are ready to do what they do best – grow, develop and learn.

This is a big issue. Public policy and expenditure are triggered by one emergency after another. A national mind-set has evolved, based on the model that the roof is leaking so we need to find ever bigger pots to catch the water. Instead we need to mend the roof.

Benefits of early attention to the three Ps

If the three Ps were writ large in Scottish policy-making, more children would grow into physically and mentally healthy adults with fulfilling lives. There would be less impoverishment and fewer scars of hurt. Poor attainment at school, children going into care, challenging behaviour and later involvement with the criminal justice system, growing mental health problems and abuse of alcohol and drugs are not different problems. They are the same problem expressed in different ways: the failure to get the first part of life right – from preconception to three years of age. What are often called 'intractable problems' are, in reality, solvable problems wrongly framed.

Doing the right thing is an end in itself. But it also helps that investing in the Ps provides the best rate of return. The Abecedarian/CARE's intervention in North Carolina[1] provided a yield of 13 per cent return on investment per child per annum throughout life. The programme provided quality intensive social-emotional support for at-risk infants and their families from birth to school age. Parents and children were engaged together in enriched learning that was tailored to be fun and affordable.

James Heckman, the Nobel Prize-winning economist who specialises in human capital, applied the same data techniques to the Perry Preschool[2] programme. This programme worked intensively for two years with three- to five-year-old disadvantaged black children, visited parents in their homes, built on how parents engaged with their children and then worked with the parents and children together. Heckman found a 7 to 10 per cent return on investment, made up from increased school and career achievement as well as reduced costs in remedial education, health and criminal justice system expenditures.

'A major determinant of successful schools is successful families,' Heckman said in a lecture in Edinburgh. 'Schools work with what parents bring them. . . Scottish skill formation policy should be based on this basic principle.'[3] The rates of return decline as children get older. Heckman identifies the highest rate of return in pregnancy, then the first months of life. The lowest rate of return is in secondary school and then university.[4]

In a time of COVID-induced radical uncertainty, the benefits of the best return on public spend become all the more important.

Holland puts Ps before Rs

In 2013, UNICEF measured child well-being in the industrialised world across twenty-six indicators. In top spot came Holland. The UK, a reasonable proxy for Scotland, was in sixteenth place, below Slovenia and the Czech Republic.[4] I asked a Dutch woman who spent the first half of her life in Holland and the second half in Scotland, why the countries differed so much in performance. 'In Holland we love children,' she told me. 'In Scotland you tolerate children.'

Holland has a great parenting culture matched by a set of relationships with sympathetic public services.[5] A *kraamzorg*, a dedicated health care professional, is selected by the mother during her pregnancy to help with the birth and the first days and, if necessary, weeks after birth. A Mother and Baby Well-being clinic is located in every community to support all parents. Also in these community facilities are Family Centres that provide intensive support for mothers and fathers who struggle most.

Across all European countries, there was a great leap in health improvement with the introduction of clean water and a sewerage system. In Holland they identified parenting as the next big public health challenge after clean water, so the Mother and Baby Well-being clinics have been a feature of life for about 110 years. This means that preparing for parenthood and contraception is part of the fabric of education and conversation in Holland. It helps that mothers and fathers tend to work part-time and share the rearing of children, aided by kith and kin. Out-sourcing or placing young children in day-care does happen but it is limited. Some teenagers make good parents but in general 'children' having children is not a good idea in Holland. Teenage parenthood in Scotland is falling but it is still 500 per cent higher than in Holland.[6]

Where are we now?

Nicola Sturgeon, First Minister of Scotland, is very clear: 'We want Scotland to be the best place in the world to bring up children.' This good intent is backed up by the rediscovery of the Health Visitor service, expansion of early learning and childcare (day-care) and the Care Review. But I fear that organisations, professionals and experts (me included) in Scotland have not done enough to frame a coherent approach, aimed at providing the real solutions.

In August 2019 a bomb went off in a blind spot. The Scottish Government hired the Scottish Centre for Social Research (ScotCen) to gather a baseline of data on two-year-old children eligible for, and receiving, 600 hours of funded childcare.[7] ScotCen collected data from parents and key workers on 574 two-year-olds, all of whom lived in households receiving certain state benefits, were looked after or in care. They were drawn from seventeen local authority areas and 151 day-care settings. Close to 50 per cent of the households were led by a single parent and 50 per cent of the households had an annual income of less than £9,701.

The good news is that two out of three parents reported that early learning and care for their children enabled them to think more about the future, a slightly smaller number felt less stressed, and just over half felt happier.

Children's key workers were asked to make observations of the child's development using the internationally recognised Ages and Stages Questionnaire (ASQ), which assesses a child's development across five life skill categories: communication, gross motor, fine motor, problem solving and personal-social. Scottish health visitors use the same questionnaire.

The results are set out in Figure 1.

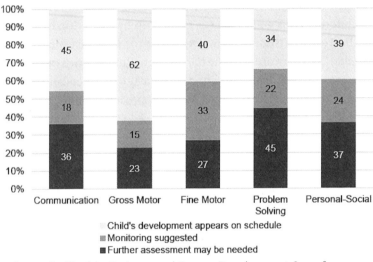

Figure 1: Eligible 2s Ages and Stages Development Score[8]

The proportion of children not meeting their developmental goals is captured in the dark part of the diagram. In fine motor skills, problem-solving and personal-social, six out of ten of the children are not meeting the expected child development standard. More than a half are behind in communication.

At this point you need to pause and let the bomb go off. If children do not have these life skills at two years of age, the foundation is missing and all their subsequent life is more likely to be impaired. **I repeat: the majority of children do not catch up.**

Mother Nature writes the rules

Mother Nature and science give us three clear messages about child development:

- Child development starts before conception and peaks from womb through to three years of age. On the down side, folic acid deficiencies, alcohol and drugs and toxic stress all create developmental problems which kick in before and during the first days and months in the womb.

- Child development is a **bottom-up process**. It's like house building, where the site, drainage, and foundation need to be right before the walls go up. Babies need a healthy pregnancy and good early sensitive attachment to thrive.

- Child development is **cumulative**. It builds, good upon good, bad upon bad. Good attachment and healthy stimulation make it easier for a child to have positive relationships, to self-regulate and to prosper at school. Neglect or a series of adverse childhood experiences make it harder for a child to learn and cope with life.

Reasons to believe

What if we monitored a thousand children of all social-economic classes between the ages of two and three, recorded their key characteristics as small children and then faithfully followed up as adults to see what happened to them at, say, 38 years of age?

We do not need to wait for the results. In 1972 in New Zealand, the Dunedin Multidisciplinary Health and Development Programme followed the entire group of children born that year in the city – just over a thousand wee souls. This group, with few dropouts, is a contender for being the most intensively studied group of people in the world. [9]

What the researchers found was that 22 per cent of the children were – when they reached the age of 38 – responsible for 81 per cent of criminal convictions, 78 per cent of prescriptions, 77 per cent of fatherless child-rearing, 66 per cent of welfare benefits and 57 per cent of hospital overnight stays.

In examining the data of the 22 per cent of the children/adults that carried the greatest burden, one predictor stood out: 'brain health' at age three. It involved a neurological examination and assessments of verbal comprehension, language development, motor skills and social behaviour. Not exactly the same assessments as the ASQ, but close enough.

The research team agreed on their most significant finding: 'Self control in childhood is more important than socio-economic status or IQ in predicting adults' physical health, wealth, life satisfaction, addiction, crime and parenting of the next generation.'

Parents and the first stage of life

Chapter 13 of this book discusses the Scottish pilot of the Early Development Instrument (EDI). To remind you, all Primary 1 pupils in East Lothian were assessed using the EDI and the results tell us that 73 per cent of them were on track.

But that means 27 out of 100 children were 'vulnerable' (i.e. the child has scored below the tenth percentile for the entire population on two or more of: social competence, emotional maturity, language and cognitive ability or physical health and well-being). Looking exclusively at the vulnerable children, almost half came from the 40 per cent of households with the lowest income. The other half of the vulnerable children came from the 60 per cent of families with middle and higher incomes.

There are two important conclusions from these quoted studies. First is the size of the challenge: around 60 per cent of 'eligible twos' (i.e. children from the financially poorest section of the population) did not meet their milestones. Each child is likely, as they grow older, to accumulate further deficits. For the country, this creates a disgraceful footprint.

Second, while more of the children from poorest households have developmental and behaviour problems, the challenge does not stop there – it is spread across all income groups. Clearly, being a good parent does not start at a certain salary level.

From Scottish government sources we know a great number of very young children are not getting a proper start. In 2017/18, a quarter of children taken into care were under twenty days old. They were being protected from 'significant harm or likelihood of significant harm'.[10] Children under the age of one are the fastest expanding group going into care. In the 'age profile of homicide victims', the under-ones are the most murdered age group in Scotland.[11]

And to return to the building metaphor, in Scotland, at age two, about one in four of all children have a crack in their gable end. Every builder who constructed a house like this would face public condemnation.

'Rithmetic of early day-care

From conception to the time of their third birthday, children live through 196 weeks and, if they take the full allocation of 1,140 funded hours of day-care, will have spent 3.6 per cent of their life in day-care. Deduct the time in the womb and the first two years of life, and total time in day-care in their third year is 13.5 per cent.

Let's think about it the other way round: by the age of three, about 90 per cent of a child's life has been spent at home with parents or carers.

There is evidence that high-quality childcare can be a supportive factor for children who live with adults who provide low-quality care. This theoretical finding was reinforced in the robust study Effective Provision of Pre-school Education (EPPE).[12] One of their findings was that 'whilst not eliminating disadvantage, pre-school can help to ameliorate the effects.'

But 'rithmetic and logic suggests that the best route is to engage with parents. It is the parents who conceive and carry the child, and who are their primary or only carer during the first two years of life, the most sensitive and profound period of growth and development.

Motivated by good intent, government policy has driven into a cul-de-sac of day-care being the answer. There is a way out and that is by building the connection with parents from birth and evolving day-care into family centres.

Right from the start

Parenting is joyous and frustrating and, like COVID, it is a public health issue. Prevention means stopping something bad happening – think COVID and early lockdown and vaccinations. Early intervention means tackling the problem before it gets out of hand and it's the smart thing to do – think COVID testing and track and trace.

What we need to focus on is parents preparing and being equipped for conception, pregnancy and the new arrival. In this way there will be fewer children with a cracked gable end at the age of two and we'll have the greatest return on public investment. Parents with greater agency, and the where-with-all to support their children, will be more likely to nurture agency and self-control in their children.

At present very few people are prepared for pregnancy or caring for a child. A driving test is compulsory before taking a car on the road and even a simple appliance like a toaster comes with a wad of instructions. Parents need support at each stage to prepare for preconception, first pregnancy, between pregnancies and the first 24 months of their child's play and development.

Preconception is the time, if your partner is beating you or you are abusing alcohol or drugs, when you need a lot of support. Folic acid needs to be taken in the months *before* pregnancy and the first month of pregnancy. In 2018 there were over 13,000 abortions in Scotland – that's a big car crash. For example, support and encouragement to take long lasting reversible contraception should be provided for women with mental health problems and/or a street drug or alcohol dependency.[13]

Pregnancy and alcohol do not mix. Exposure to alcohol before birth is the most important preventable cause of brain damage in children. Alcohol is teratogenic, a substance that readily crosses the placenta, causing cell death or inhibiting cell growth.

The foetus is unprotected from alcohol circulating in the blood system.[14] A recent study in Glasgow found 42 per cent of mothers had taken alcohol during pregnancy, with 15 per cent of those pregnancies exposed to very high levels of alcohol.[15] This is before considering the damage to early cells and foetuses caused by street and prescription drugs and/or domestic violence, which some evidence suggests peaks in pregnancy.

Support for parenting has practical implications, which are affected by cultural assumptions. Let's briefly look at two examples. First, the Baby Box in Scotland is made up of goods and an advice leaflet, delivered by the postman, to the mother late in the pregnancy. In Finland, where the Baby Box originated, it is part of a much fuller approach to engaging the prospective parents in their new role.

Second, many parents are buckled by the burden of how they themselves were neglectfully or abusively parented. Preparing for parenthood provides a golden opportunity for reflecting on and tackling these issues. Trained play therapists know how to do this, as do many people trained in delivering pregnancy and parenting programmes.

Parent power and the power of play
Parents are the constant and biggest influence on a child's life, providing attachment and sensitive care – or not. Too often, the role of the parent is viewed as 'technical' – going for an ultrasound during pregnancy; opening the door to the postman when the Baby Box comes; conveying the child to and from the day-care provider. All parents of young children struggle and particularly, but not exclusively, parents damaged by their own upbringing are 'not waving but drowning'. In reviews of early

childhood programmes, the approaches that are most effective and bring the greatest return on money spent, work with the children, engage the parents and work with parents and children together.

Play is essential and is what young children do – mimicking sounds and actions, finding how limbs and fingers work, exploring and expressing. Children can be a challenge but they're also fun and can light up everyone's life. Part of the 'tolerating children' mentality is to see young children like electric cars: ready to be plugged into an electric socket or day-care and school. Loving children means giving full attention to preconception, pregnancy, parenting and play for these first few vital years of life.

One day, Scotland will finally realise the immense significance of early child development – not just for the children themselves, but for our society as a whole. When that day comes, we'll start supporting all parents to provide high-quality care for their children until they're around three years old.

By three, they need to play and learn with other children – and parents usually need to return to work or go part-time. A relationship-centred, play-based kindergarten stage until the age of seven is a natural building block. By the time the children start school they will have developed self-regulation skills – that critical 'self control' identified by Dunedin – and the vast majority will soon have the three Rs under their belts and be ready to thrive.

But please remember that for everyone's personal and collective benefit, P comes before R. ☐

References

Chapter 1

1 Quoted in Knox, W.W. (2000) The Scottish Educational System 1840 – 1940. *A History of the Scottish People.* https://www.scran.ac.uk/scotland/pdf/SP2_1Education.pdf

2 Knox, W.W. (2000) as above

3 Tour Scotland website: https://tour-scotland-photographs.blogspot.com/2018/08/old-photograph-boys-and-girls-at-school.html

4 *Scottish Daily Mail* (2014) Shame of schools which fail our children. 19-6-14

5 *Scotland is Now* website: https://www.scotland.org/live-in-scotland/school-systems

6 eg., Knox, W.W. (2000) see 1 above and Smout, T.C. (1987) *A Century of the Scottish People: 1830 – 1950.* (Harper Collins)

7 Knox, W.W. (2000) see 1 above

8 Upstart Scotland website: https://www.upstart.scot/reasons/

9 *The Herald.* (2020) Coronavirus: Plan to help pupils get in touch with emotions. 27-7 20

10 *Glasgow Evening Times.* Row as private nurseries claim children are being 'uprooted' due to North Lanarkshire Council funding decisions. 10-8-20

11 McFadden, J. (2016) Growing up in an ultra-strict church. *The Guardian.* 10 September 2016

12 Knox, W.W. (2000) see 1 above

13 Knox, W.W. (2000) see 1 above

14 Fifty years of nurture in policy. Nurture UK website: https://www.nurtureuk.org/50-years-nurture/50-years-nurture-policy

15 March, S. & Kearney, M. (2017) A psychological service contribution to nurture: Glasgow's nurturing city. *Emotional and Behavioural Difficulties*, 22(3), 237-247

16 KPJR Films. (2016) *Resilience: The biology of stress and the science of hope*. Documentary film. Trailer can be viewed on this link: https://vimeo.com/137282528

17 Craig, C. (2018) Scotland's 'addiction to the belt'. *Sceptical Scot blog series*. https://sceptical.scot/2018/04/scotlands-addiction-belt/

18 End All Corporal Punishment of Children website: https://endcorporalpunishment.org/countdown/

19 McKaveney, D. (2020) Strengthening children's rights in Scotland. *Human Rights blog series*. https://ukhumanrightsblog.com/2020/03/24/strengthening-childrens-rights-in-scotland/

20 Wood, E. (2020) Delivering on a promise: The Independent Care Review. *Holyrood Magazine*

21 Scottish Government. (2020) *Realising the Ambition: Being Me. National Practice Guidance for Early Years in Scotland.* Accessible on Scottish Government website. https://education.gov.scot/improvement/learning-resources/realising-the-ambition/

22 Palmer, S. (2020) 'Realising the ambition' in a time of coronavirus. *Sceptical Scot blog series*. https://sceptical.scot/2020/05/realising-the-ambition-in-a-time-of-coronavirus/

23 More information can be found on the Circle of Security International website: www.circleofsecurityinternational.com

24 Circle of Security Parenting Video. (2010) Archived on

YouTube. https://www.youtube.com/watch?v=cW2BfxsWguc

25 Carnochan, J. (2018) 'What is stopping us?' Keynote address for Upstart AGM. Archived on YouTube. https://www.youtube.com/watch?v=mk7H_GQ7Gpg&list=PLMGHHdba9X1_d7K-opc-UOAX5cBwc0es6&index=2&t=0s

Chapter 2

1 Rousseau, J.J. (1762) *Emile or On Education*

2 UNESCO website (2017) https://en.unesco.org/themes/early-childhood-care-and-education Accessed 24/8/20

3 Lester, S. & Russell, W. (2008) *Play for a Change: Summary report* (Play England)

4 Isaacs, S. (1929) *The Nursery Years* (Routledge)

5 Sturrock, G. Russell, W. and Else, P. (2004) *Towards Ludogogy: Parts I, 11 & 111* (Ludemos)

6 Edwards c et al (2011) *The Hundred Languages of Children: The Reggio Emilia Approach-Advanced Reflections* (Praeger)

7 Vallatton, C. and Ayoub, C. (2011) Use your words: The role of language in the development of toddlers' self-regulation. *Early Childhood Research Quarterly*

8 Whitebread, D. (2011) *Developmental Psychology and Early Childhood Education* (Sage)

9 Lester, S. & Russell, W. (2008) *Play for a Change: Summary report* (Play England)

10 Cole-Hamilton, I. (2012) *Getting it Right for Play: The Power of Play: an evidence base* (Play Scotland)

11 Gill, T. (2014) *The Play Return: A review of the wider impacts of play initiatives* (Play Scotland)

12 Scottish Government (2013) *Play Strategy for Scotland: Our Vision* (Scottish Government)

13 UNCRC (1989) *The United Nations Convention on the Rights of the Child* (UNICEF)

14 UNCRC (2013) *General comment No.17 on the right of the child to rest, leisure, play, recreational activities, cultural life and the arts* London (UNICEF)

15 UNCRC (2013) as 14 above

16 UNCRC (2013) as 14 above

17 Hughes, B. (2002) *A playworker's taxonomy of play types* (Playlink)

18 Whitebread, D. Dr. (2012) *The importance of play: A report on the value of children's play with a series of policy recommendations* (Cambridge Scholars Publishing)

19 Scottish Government (2008) *The Early Years Framework* Edinburgh (Scottish Government)

20 Play Strategy, see 12 above

21 Scottish Government (2019) *Planning (Scotland) Act 2019* Edinburgh: Scottish Government

22 The Scottish Executive (2007) *A curriculum for excellence: Building the Curriculum 2 – Active learning in the early years* (Scottish Executive)

23 Scottish Government (2014) *Building the Ambition: National Practice Guidance on Early Learning and Childcare* (Scottish Government)

24 Education Scotland (2020) *Realising the Ambition: Being Me* (Education Scotland)

25 Education Scotland *Play Pedagogy Toolkit* accessed online 23/8/20 www.education.gov.scot/improvement/learning-resources/early-level-play-pedagogy-toolkit/

26 Newcastle University *Gateshead Millennium Study* accessed online 23/8/20 https://research.ncl.ac.uk/gms/

27 Casey, T. and Robertson, J. (2019) *Loose Parts Play Toolkit 2nd edition* (Inspiring Scotland)

28 Play Scotland *Playful Pedagogy Toolkit* (2020) accessed online 23/8/20 www.playscotland.org/playful-pedagogy/

Chapter 3

1 Singer, P. (1999) *A Darwinian left: Politics, evolution and cooperation,* page 61 (Weidenfeld and Nicolson)

2 Harvard Centre on the Developing Child (ND) *Brain Architecture* https://developingchild.harvard.edu/science/key-concepts/brain-architecture/ Accessed 10-10-19

3 Lemov, D. (2010) *Teach Like a Champion* (Jossey Bass).

4 Crone, A. and Ridderinkhof, R. (2011) The developing brain: From theory to neuroimaging and back. *Developmental Cognitive Neuroscience* 1 101–109

5 Piaget, J. and Inhelder, B. (1969) *The Psychology of the Child* (Basic Books)

6 Whitebread, D. and Basilio, M. 2012. The Emergence and Early Development of Self-Regulation in Young Children. *Professorado* 16:1, 15-33

7 PBS (2012) The Secret Life of the Brain: the baby's brain. YouTube. https://www.youtube.com/watch?v=MS5HUDVNbGs&feature=emb_logo Accessed 7-12-19

8 Keister, E. (2001) Accents are Forever. *The Smithsonian Magazine*. www.smithsonianmag.com/science-nature/accents-are-forever-35886605/Accessed 6-12-20

9 Brown, T. T., & Jernigan, T. L. (2012). Brain development during the preschool years. *Neuropsychology Review*, 22(4) 313–333.–https://doi.org/10.1007/s11065-012-9214-1

10 Tierney, A. L., & Nelson, C. A., 3rd (2009). Brain Development and the Role of Experience in the Early Years. *Zero to three* 30 (2), 9–13

11 Tierney & Nelson, see 10 above, page 12

12 Raymond, C, Marin, M. Majeur, D & Lupien, S (2018) Early child adversity and psychopathology in adulthood: HPA axis and cognitive dysregulations as potential mechanisms *Prog Neuropsychopharmaclo Biol Psychiatry* 13:85 152-160

13 Wagner, S. Cepeda, I., Krieger, D., Maggi, S.D'Angiulli, A., Weinberg, J. & Grunau, R. (2016) Higher cortisol is associated with poorer executive functioning in preschool children: The role of parenting stress, parent coping and quality of daycare. *Child Neuropsychology* 22 (7), 853–869

14 *Realising the Ambition,* Education Scotland, 2020

15 Owen, R. (1991) *A New View of Society and Other Writings*. London: Penguin Classics

Chapter 4

1 UN Commission on Human Rights (1990) United Nations Convention on the Rights of the Child (1990) https://www.refworld.org/docid/3b00f03d30.html Accessed 23-6-20

2 Children's Parliament: https://www.childrensparliament.org.uk/

3 United Nations Committee on the Rights of the Child (2005) *UNCRC General Comment No 7: Implementing child rights in early childhood*

4 Lundy, L (2019) A Lexicon for Research on International Children's Rights in Troubled Times' International Journal of Children's Rights *International Journal of Children's Rights* 27:4

Chapter 5

1 Isaacs, S. (2013, 1937). The educational value of the nursery school. London, England: *The British Association for Early Childhood Education*, p 10/11

2 Scottish Government (2020) *Support for Learning: All our children and all their potential.* Retrieved July 12, 2020 from: https://www.gov.scot/publications/review-additional-support-learning-implementation/

3 Scottish Government (2004). *Education (Additional Support for Learning) (Scotland) Act 2004.* http://www.legislation.gov.uk/asp/2004/4/pdfs/asp_20040004_en.pdf

4 Scottish Government (2017) *Support for children's learning: statutory guidance on the Education (Support for Learning) Scotland Act 2004*

5 Scottish Government (2017), see 4 above

6 Ahmed, S. (2014). *The cultural politics of emotion.* 2nd edn. (Edinburgh University Press)

7 Pascal, C., Bertram, T., Cullinane, C. and Holt-White, E. (2020). *COVID-19 and Social Mobility. Impact Brief #4: Early Years* (The Sutton Trust)

8 Nutbrown, C. and Clough, P. (2010). Citizenship and inclusion in the early years: understanding and responding to children's perspectives on 'belonging', *International Journal of Early Years Education,* 17:3, 191-206

9 Woodhead, M. and Brooker, L. (2008). A sense of belonging. *Early Childhood Matters: enhancing a sense of belonging in the early years,* p.3-6 (Bernard Van Leer Foundation)

10 Scottish Government (2020) see 2 above.

11 Nutbrown, C. (2018). *Early childhood educational research: international perspectives.* London, England: SAGE Publications Ltd.

12 Te Pou o te Whakaaro Nui (2019). *Te Tao Tītoki: a framework for supporting people on the autism spectrum* p5 (Te Pou o te Whakaaro Nui)

13 Nutbrown, C. (1996). Wide eyes and open minds – observing, assessing and respecting children's early achievements. In C. Nutbrown (Ed.) *Respectful educators – capable learners: children's rights and early education.* (Paul Chapman)

14 Henderson, E. (2018). *Autoethnography in early childhood education and care: narrating the heart of practice.* (Routledge)

15 Noddings, 2002 quoted in Andresen, R. (2013). Visions of what inclusive education can be – with emphasis on kindergartens. *European Early Childhood Education Research Journal*, 21:3, 392-406

16 Unwin, J. (2018) *Kindness, emotions and human relationships: The blind spot in public policy* (Carnegie Trust UK)

Chapter 8

1 Deferral Support Scotland: https://www.facebook.com/groups/1680426968699639/

2 Education [Scotland] Act 1980: section 32, sub-section 3. Accessed 26/8/20: https://www.legislation.gov.uk/ukpga/1980/44/section/32

3 Give Them Time – www.givethemtime.org and Twitter @GiveTimeScot

Chapter 9

1 Hempenstall, K (2012) *Literacy and mental health* (updated 2018) National Institute for Direct Instruction, Oregon USA https://www.nifdi.org/news-latest-2/blog-hempenstall/404-literacy-and-mental-health

2 Castles, A., Rastle, K., & Nation, K. (2018). Ending the reading wars: Reading acquisition from novice to expert. *Psychological Science in the Public Interest*, 19, 5–51

3 Gibb, N (2015) *The Importance of Phonics* Department for Education accessed 25/8/20: https://www.gov.uk/government/speeches/nick-gibb-the-importance-of-phonics

4 Rohde, L (2015) The Comprehensive Emergent Literacy Model: Early Literacy in Context (Sage Open) accessed 25/8/20: https://journals.sagepub.com/doi/pdf/10.1177/2158244015577664

5 World Bank *School Starting Age (Years) All countries and economies* (2020) accessed 25/8/20: https://data.worldbank.org/indicator/SE.PRM.AGES

6 Palmer, S (2016) *Upstart: the case for raising the school starting age and providing what the under-sevens really need* Chapter 6 (Floris Books)

7 Harvard Centre for the Developing Child *Key Concept: Serve and Return* accessed 25-8-20: https://developingchild.harvard.edu/science/key-concepts/serve-and-return/

8 Bruce T and Spratt J (2011) *Essentials of Literacy from 0 to 7* (Sage)

9 Wolf, M (2006) *Proust and the Squid: the story and science of the reading brain* (Icon)

10 Bertrand T and Pascal C (2018) 'Why Children's Dispositions Should Matter to All Teachers' (US Department of Health and Human Studies) Accessed 25/8/20: https://eclkc.ohs.acf.hhs.gov/school-readiness/article/why-childrens-dispositions-should-matter-all-teachers

11 Pascal C, Bertrand T and Rouse L (2019) *Getting It Right In the EYFS* (British Association for Early Childhood Education Research Association)

12 Purdon A (2014) 'Sustained shared thinking in an early childhood setting: an exploration of practitioners' perspectives' *Education 3-13*

13 Bruce T, McNair, L, Whinnett J eds (2020) *Putting Storytelling at the Heart of Early Childhood Practice* (Routledge)

14 Sosu E and Ellis S (2014) *Closing the Attainment Gap in Scottish Schools* (Joseph Rowntree Foundation)

15 Suggate S et al, (2013) 'Children learning to read later catch up children reading earlier' in *Early Childhood Research Quarterly 28*

16 Marcon, R (2002) 'Moving up the Grades: Relationship between Preschool Model and Later School Success' *Early Childhood Research & Practice 4:1*

17 Schweinhart L and Weikart DP (1993) *Lasting Differences: The High/Scope Preschool Curriculum Comparison Study through Age 27* (High/Scope Press)

18 Kern M and Friedman HS (2008) Early educational milestones as predictors of life-long academic achievement, mid-life adjustment, and longevity *Journal of Applied Developmental Psychology* (as part of the Longevity Project)

19 Carlton Paige N, McLaughlin GB, Almon JW (2013) *Reading Instruction in Kindergarten: nothing to gain and much to lose* (Alliance for Childhood)

20 e.g. Gray, P (2011) The Decline of Play and the Rise of Psychopathology in Children and Adolescents *American Journal of Play, 3;4*

21 Scottish Government (2004) *Curriculum for Excellence*

22 Education Scotland (2020) *Realising the Ambition: Being Me*

Chapter 10

1 Scottish Office Education Department (1991) *Mathematics 5-14 National Guidelines* (The Scottish Executive)

2 Thiel O & Perry B (2018) Innovative approaches in early childhood mathematics *European Early Childhood Education Research Journal*, 26:4

3 Education Endowment Foundation (2019) Improving Mathematics in the Early Years and Key Stage 1 3 Guidance Report https://educationendowmentfoundation.org.uk/tools/guidance-reports/early-maths/

4 Education Scotland (2020) *Realising the Ambition: Being Me*

5 National Centre for Excellence in the Teaching of Mathematics: https://www.ncetm.org.uk

6 Turnaround for Children: https://www.turnaroundusa.org/what-we-do/tools/building-blocks/

7 Ephgrave A (2017) *Year One in Action: a month-by-month guide to taking Early Years pedagogy into KS1* (David Fulton)

8 Maths through Stories https://www.mathsthroughstories.org

9 Jay T and Betenson J (2017) Mathematics at Your Fingertips: Testing a Finger Training Intervention to Improve Quantitative Skills. *Front. Educ.* 2:22

10 Nicholson, S. (1971) How NOT to Cheat Children: The Theory of Loose Parts *Landscape Architecture*, 62, 30-34. Accessed 13/06/20 at: https:// media.kaboom.org/docs/documents/pdf/ip/ Imagination-Playground-Theory-of-Loose-Parts-Simon-Nicholson.pdf

11 Haylock, D. and Cockburn, A. (2013).*Understanding Mathematics for Young Children: A Guide for Teachers of Children 3–8*, 4th edn (Sage)

Chapter 11

1 Scottish Government (2008) *The Early Years Framework*, (Scottish Government) Available at: https://www2.gov.scot/ Publications/2009/01/13095148/

2 Scottish Social Services Council: https://www.sssc.uk.com/ registration/

3 General Teaching Council for Scotland: https:// www.gtcs.org.uk/

4 Dunlop, A-W, Frame, K., Goodier, J., Miles, C., Renton, K. & Small, M. with Adie, J. & Ludke, K. (2016). *Sustaining the Ambition: The contribution of GTCS-registered teachers as part of the early learning and childcare workforce in Scotland* (The Child's Curriculum Group)

5 Siraj, I and Kingston, D. (2015). An Independent Review of the Scottish Early Learning and Childcare (ELC) Workforce and Out of School Care (OSC) Workforce. (UCL Institute of Education)

6 General Teaching Council for Scotland: https://www.gtcs.org.uk/

7 Education Scotland, (2020) *Realising the Ambition: Being Me*

8 Nicholson, J., Kuhl, K., Maniates. H., Lin, B. and Sara Bonetti, S. (2020). A review of the literature on leadership in early childhood: examining epistemological foundations and considerations of social justice, *Early Child Development and Care,* 190, 2, 91-122

9 Sylva, K., Melhuish, E., Sammons, P., Siraj, I., Taggart, B., Smees, R., Hollingworth, K. (2014). Effective Pre-School, Primary and Secondary Education (EPPSE 3-16) Project: Students' educational and developmental outcomes at age 16. (Department for Education)

10 e.g. Rinaldi, C. (2013). Re-imagining Childhood, The Inspiration of Reggio Emelia Principles in South Australia (Government of South Australia)

11 Education Scotland (2020) *Realising the Ambition*

12 Education Scotland (2020) *Realising the Ambition,* p6

13 Marie Todd (2020) Ministerial Foreword in *Realising the Ambition* (see above)

14 Carey, J., & Karagiannidou, E. (2016). *An Evaluation of The Early Years Pedagogue Masters (Phase 1)* (University of Strathclyde)

15 Bruce, T., McNair, L. and Whinnett, J. (2020). *Putting Storytelling at the Heart of Early Childhood Practice* (Routledge)

16 Dunlop, A-W (2020). A Study of Leadership in the Early Years in Scotland (in progress)

17 Menter, I., Elliot, D., Hulme, M., Lewin, J., and Lowden, K. (2011) *A Guide to Practitioner Research in Education* (Sage)

18 Gilchrist, G (2018). *Practitioner Enquiry: Professional Development with Impact for Teachers, Schools and Systems* (Routledge)

19 Scottish Government (2018). A Blueprint for 2020: The Expansion of Early Learning and Childcare in Scotland 2017 – 2018 Action Plan

20 Froebel, F. (1896). *The Education of Man* (translated by W.N. Hailmann) (Appleton)

21 Vasinova, I. (2020) *Follow Me if You Can.* BA Childhood Practice Conference Poster Presentation, University of Edinburgh

22 McNair, L.J. (2012) 'Offering Children First-Hand Experiences Through Forest School: Relating to and Learning About Nature'. In T. Bruce (ed.) *Froebel Today* (Sage)

23 Carr, M. and Lee, W. (2012). Learning Stories: Constructing Learner Identities in Early Education London: Sage. And Carr, M. and Lee, W. (2019). Learning Stories in Practice (Sage)

24 Scottish Social Services Council (2020). Strategic Plan 2020-2023. (SSSC)

Chapter 12

1 Scottish Government (2004) *Curriculum for Excellence*

2 Education Scotland (2020) *Realising the Ambition: Being Me*

3 Scotland's Futures Forum and Goodison Group in Scotland (2020) *Schooling, Education and Learning – 2030 and beyond.* (SFF & GGIS)

4 Pascal C, Bertrand T and Rouse L (2019) *Getting It Right In the EYFS* (British Association for Early Childhood Education Research Association)

5 Purdon A (2014) 'Sustained shared thinking in an early childhood setting: an exploration of practitioners' perspectives' *Education 3-13*

6 World Economic Forum (2018) *The Future of Jobs Report* (WEF)

7 Dee T and Sievertsen HH (2018) 'The gift of time? School starting age and mental health' *Health Economics 27;5*

8 e.g. Harris JR (1998) *The Nurture Assumption* (Free Press)

9 Yogman M, Garner A, et al (2018) 'The Power of Play: A Pediatric Role in Enhancing Development' *Pediatrics*, 142 (3)

Chapter 13

1 World Health Organization. (2008). *Final report for the WHO's Commission on Social Determinants of Health* (World Health Organization)

2 Irwin, L. G., Siddiqi, A., & Hertzman, C. (2007).*Early child development: A powerful equalizer.* Final report for the WHO's Commission on Social Determinants of Health (World Health Organization)

3 Figure 1: from: Total environment assessment model for early child development: Evidence report for the Commission on Social Determinants of Health (p. 15), by A. Siddiqi, L. G. Irwin, and C. Hertzman, 2007 (World Health Organization) Reprinted with permission of the authors

4 Irwin et al. 2007 (see 2 above), p. 151

5 McCain, M., & Mustard, J. (1999) *Reversing the Real Brain Drain: Early Years Study. Final Report.* Toronto: Publications Ontario; Shonkoff, J., & Phillips, D. (2000). *From Neurons to Neighbourhoods: The Science of Early Childhood Development.* (National Academy Press)

6 Heckman, J. (2006). Skill formation and the economics of investing in disadvantaged children. *Science, 312*, 1900-1902; Marmot, M. (2010). *Fair Society, Healthy Lives*. (University College London)

7 Ludwig, J., Phillips, D. (2007) The benefits and costs of head start *Social Policy Report*, 21, 3-19

8 Offord Centre for Child Studies, McMaster University, Canada, 2019 https://edi.offordcentre.com/about/what-is-the-edi/ (Figure 2 is adapted from this summary)

9 Janus, M., & Offord, D. (2007). Psychometric properties of the Early Development Instrument (EDI): A teacher-completed measure of children's readiness to learn at school entry. *Canadian Journal of Behavioural Science, 39*(1), 1–22

10 Kershaw, P., Irwin, L., Trafford, K., & Hertzman, C. (2005) The British Columbia atlas of child development, Human Early Learning Partnership, *Canadian Western Geographical Series, 40;* Hertzman, C. (2010) Tackling inequality: get them while they're young, *British Medical Journal, 340,* 346-348

11 Brinkman, S. A., Gregory, T. A., Goldfeld, S., Lynch, J. W., & Hardy, M. (2014). Data resource profile: the Australian early development index (AEDI). *International Journal of Epidemiology, 43*(4), 1089-1096

12 Woolfson LM, Geddes R, McNicol S, Booth J, Frank JW. (2013). A cross-sectional pilot study of the Scottish Early Development Instrument: A tool for addressing inequality *BMC Public Health* 201

13 Hardie S. (2014). A qualitative study examining the influence of the Early Development Instrument in East Lothian (University of Edinburgh)

14 Scottish Government (2020). *Long-term Monitoring of Health Inequalities: January 2020 Report.* Available at: https://www.gov.scot/publications/long-term-monitoring-health-inequalities-january-2020-report/ [Accessed July 2020]

15 Heckman 2006 (see 6 above)

16 Hertzman C, Vaghri Z, Arkadas-Thibert A. (2013). Monitoring progress toward fulfilling rights in early childhood under the Convention on the Rights of the Child to improve outcomes for children and families. In: Britto, P. R., Engle, P. L., & Super, C. M. (Eds.). (2013). *Handbook of Early Childhood Development Research and its Impact on Global Policy* (Oxford University Press)

17 UNCRC (1989) Convention on the Rights of the Child. [Online] https://www.ohchr.org/en/professionalinterest/pages/crc.aspx [Accessed July 2020]

18 UNCRC (2005) Implementing child rights in early childhood (General Comment 7). [Online] https://www.ohchr.org/_layouts/15/WopiFrame.aspx?sourcedoc=/Documents/Issues/Women/WRGS/Health/GC7.pdf&action=default&DefaultItemOpen=1 [Accessed July 2020]

Chapter 14

1 The Carolina Abecedarian Project *The Abecedarian Project* accessed 27/8/20 https://abc.fpg.unc.edu/abecedarian-project

2 Social Programmes That Work *The Perry Preschool Project* accessed 27/8/20: https://evidencebasedprograms.org/programs/perry-preschool-project/

3 Coyle D, Alexander W and Ashcroft B (2005) *New Wealth for Old Nations* (Princeton University Press)

4 Heckman J and Masterov DV, *Skill Policies for Scotland* (University of Chicago) http://jenni.uchicago.edu/papers/allander_as_printed.pdf

5 UNICEF (2013) *Child well-being in rich countries: A comparative overview*: *UNICEF, Innocenti Report Card 11*

6 Acosta RM and Hutchison M (2017) *The Happiest Kids in the World: Bringing up children the Dutch way* (Doubleday)

7 SenScot (2019) *Scottish Study of Early Learning and Childcare: Phase 1 Report* (Scottish Government)

8 Figure 1: from Senscot (2019) – see 7 above

9 Poulton, R., Moffitt T.E., & Silva, P.A., 2015. 'The Dunedin Multidisciplinary Health and Development Study: Overview of the 40 years with an eye to the future' *Social Psychiatry and Psychiatric Epidemiology*

10 Scottish Government (2019) *Children's Social Work Statistics, 2017-18* Accessed 27/8/20: https://www.gov.scot/publications/childrens-social-work-statistics-2017-2018/

11 Scottish Government (2018) *Homicide in Scotland, 2017-18, Statistics* Accessed 27/8/20: https://www.gov.scot/publications/homicide-scotland-2017-18/pages/4/

12 Sylva K, Melhuish E, Sammons P, Siraj-Blatchford I, Taggart B (2004) *The Effective Provision of Pre-School Education (EPPE) Project: findings from pre-school to end of Key Stage 1*

Accessed 27/8/20 https://dera.ioe.ac.uk/8543/7/SSU-SF-2004-01.pdf

13 Centre on the Developing Child (2017) In Brief series: *Early Childhood Mental Health; The Foundation of Mental Health; The Science of Early Childhood Development* (Harvard University)

14 Sher J (2016) *Missed Periods: Scotland's Opportunities for Better Pregnancies.* (NHS Greater Glasgow and Clyde Public Health)

15 Healthcare Improvement Scotland (2019) *Children and young people exposed prenatally to alcohol* (Scottish Intercollegiate Guidelines Network -SIGN publication 156)

About the Contributors

Patricia Anderson has worked in education for over twenty years as a foreign language teacher, secondary English teacher and now in widening participation at a Scottish university. She became interested in the debate around Scotland's early school starting age as a parent, having deferred both of her children's primary one starts for very different reasons.

Dr Marion Burns HMI now works part time with Education Scotland. Her area of expertise is early learning and childcare – more specifically play pedagogy and children's transition to school. She is a co-author of *Realising the Ambition: Being Me,* the national practice guidance for early years in Scotland. She is a wife, mum, and nannie to Ben and Beth.

Diane Delaney spent 15 years as a care manager in social work services. She is currently studying the experiences of parents concerned about their four-year-olds transitioning to primary school, as part of a Masters degree in Public Health. Her interest in the subject stems from experience of deferring her own child's entry to school, with the assistance of Upstart supporters.

Professor Aline-Wendy Dunlop has worked variously in early childhood, primary and special education, a residential home for mothers and babies, as a home-visiting teacher, a nursery head and a teacher educator and researcher. Now Emeritus Professor at the University of Strathclyde, she continues to research and write, and to play and learn with her grandchildren.

John Frank is Professor of Public Health, Usher Institute, University of Edinburgh and Professor Emeritus, Dalla Lana School of Public Health, University of Toronto, Toronto, Canada.

Dr Rosemary Geddes is Programme Co-Director Master of Public Health (online), Usher Institute, University of Edinburgh and Research Associate, African Centre for Migration & Society, University of the Witwatersrand, South Africa.

Dr Elizabeth Henderson has worked in the field of education and care for over 40 years in a variety of contexts, from nursery to university. She currently works in a Scottish local authority supporting ELC professionals and is engaged in building a Community of Practice in outdoor ELC. Elizabeth also explores the multi-layered context that is ELC practice, in her personal writing and research.

Marguerite Hunter Blair is Chief Executive of Play Scotland, the national play organisation (since 2006). A leading figure championing the child's right to play, she was previously CEO of PlayBoard Northern Ireland, after a career in community development with Belfast City Council.

Dr Pam Jarvis is a chartered psychologist, historian and qualified teacher. After a career in academia, she is currently Honorary Research Fellow at Leeds Trinity University. Her extensive academic publishing includes

'Perspectives on Play.' She blogs in various media including the *TES* and *Yorkshire Bylines* and is working on her first novel, which explores her Scottish ancestry (working title *On Time*).

Kate Johnson is a retired nursery teacher and Vice-Chair of Upstart Scotland. A Froebelian since Primary 1, where she was taught by Mary Beaton, and later inspired by Sheena Johnstone at Moray House, she is honoured to have watched as play has become the way in many Scottish schools.

Sarah Latto is Manager of the Secret Garden Outdoor Nursery in Fife, having previously worked as a ranger in the highlands and supporting the development of an outdoor nursery. Her background is in ecology and she has a Masters in Outdoor, Environmental and Sustainability Education.

Lisa McCabe is Education Team Manager at Falkirk Council. She has strategic leadership responsibility for the quality improvement of early learning across early learning and childcare and early stages of primary school.

Cathy McCulloch OBE works mainly in the field of education and human rights. Following an international environmental education project in 1992 where children said 'we need a children's parliament, a place where adults take us seriously', Cathy co-founded The Children's Parliament in Scotland with Dr Colin Morrison. They are now Co-Directors.

Dr Lynn McNair is Head of Cowgate Under Fives Centre in Edinburgh, Scotland and a Senior Teaching Fellow at the

University of Edinburgh. A trained Froebelian with 30 years' experience working in early years education, she was awarded an OBE for services to early education in 2009.

Sue Palmer is a former primary head teacher, literacy consultant and author whose interest in child development arose through research for *Toxic Childhood*, *21st Century Boys* and *21st Century Girls* and led to publication of *Upstart: the case for raising the school starting age.* She was a founding member of Upstart Scotland (www.upstart.scot) and is now its Chair.

Juliet Robertson is an education consultant who specialises in providing support, training, advice and resources about outdoor learning and play at a local and national level. She is the author of *Dirty Teaching: A Beginner's Guide to Learning Outdoors* and *Messy Maths: A Playful, Outdoor Approach for Early Years.*

Alan Sinclair was Chief Executive of Heatwise Glasgow and the Wise Group, pioneering ways of getting long-term unemployed people into work. Subsequently he was the Senior Director for Skills and Learning for Scottish Enterprise. In 2000 he was awarded a CBE. His book *Right from the Start: Investing in parents and babies* is another in the Postcard series.

Dr Suzanne Zeedyk is a developmental psychologist based for 20 years at the University of Dundee, before setting out in 2011 to disseminate 'the science of connection' to the public. She is Founder of the organisation *Connected Baby* (www.connectedbaby.net), and a leading voice in the ACE-aware movement in Scotland.

Other books in the series

1. AfterNow – What next for a healthy Scotland?
| *Phil Hanlon/Sandra Carlisle*
The authors of this visionary book look at health in Scotland and beyond health to the main social, economic, environmental and cultural challenges of our times. They examine the type of transformational change required to create a more resilient and healthy Scotland.

2. The Great Takeover – How materialism, the media and markets now dominate our lives | *Carol Craig*
Describes the dominance of materalist values, the media and business in all our lives and how this is leading to a loss of individual and collective well-being. It looks at many of the big issues of our times – debt, inequality, political apathy, loss of self-esteem, pornography and the rise of celebrity culture. The conclusion is simple and ultimately hopeful – we can change our values and our lives.

3. The New Road – Charting Scotland's inspirational communities
| *Alf Young/Ewan Young*
A father and son go on a week long journey round Scotland to see at first hand some of the great environmental, social, employment and regeneration projects which are happening. From Dunbar in the south east of Scotland to Knoydart in the north west they meet people involved in projects which demonstrate new ways of living.

4. Scotland's Local Food Revolution | *Mike Small*
Lifts the lid on the unsavoury reality of our current food system including horsemeat in processed beef products, the unsustainable

movement of food round the globe, and how supermarket shopping generates massive waste. It's an indictment of a food syste that is out of control. But there is hope – the growth and strength of Scotland's local food movement.

5. Letting Go – Breathing new life into organisations
| *Tony Miller/Gordon Hall*
It is now commonplace for employees to feel frustrated at work – ground down by systems that are dominated by rules, protocols, guidelines, targets and inspections. Tony Miller and Gordon Hall explore the origins of 'command and control' management as well as the tyranny of modern day 'performance management'. Effective leaders, they argue, should 'let go' of their ideas on controlling staff and nurture intrinsic motivation instead.

6. Raising Spirits – Allotments, well-being and community | *Jenny Mollison/Judy Wilkinson/Rona Wilkinson*
Allotments are the unsung story of our times; hidden places for food, friendship and freedom from the conformity of everyday life. A fascinating look at how allotments came about; why they can make such a substantial contribution to health, well-being, community, food production, and the environment; and what's happening in other countries.

7. Schooling Scotland – Education, equity and community | *Daniel Murphy*
The Scottish schooling system does well for many children growing up in Scotland, but to ensure that all children get the education they deserve, a better partnership of parent, child, school, government and society is needed – one to which all Scotland can contribute and from which all children can benefit. Daniel Murphy suggests eight ways to ensure that Scottish education could be stronger and fairer.

8. Shaping our Global Future – A guide for young people | *Derek Brown*
Young people worry about the future world they will live in: personal futures, families and jobs. But they also worry about their global futures. The possibilities and challenges ahead appear overwhelming. This guide to human achievements and future challenges is designed to help young people consider the future their children and grandchildren will inhabit.

9. Conviction – Violence, culture and a shared public service agenda | *John Carnochan*
Policeman John Carnochan takes us on a memorable journey of discovery as he comes to grips with violence and Scotland's traditionally high murder rate. He also gives a fascinating insight into the work of Scotland's Violence Reduction Unit and why it has been so spectacularly successful. This compelling book is not about high visibility policing or more officers but the importance of empathy and children's early years.

10. She, He, They – Families, gender and coping with transition | *Shirley Young*
How challenging can gender transition be for both parents and siblings? A story of hope and resilience, it shows that if parents can move beyond the shock and pain of their offspring's transition, all family members can come closer together and experience life-enhancing change.

11. Knowing and Growing – Insights for developing ourselves and others | *Alan McLean*
This extraordinary book provides insights and practical tools to help you navigate everyday human interactions, balance your own and others' needs and utilise your emotions to create a more fulfilling life. The powerful insights readers glean from 'McLean's Ring' are not only helpful for parents, teachers and leaders they are also essential for anyone aiming to encourage others to grow and develop as individuals.

12. Working for Equality – Policy, politics people |
Richard Freeman, Fiona McHardy, Danny Murphy (Editors)
Brings together 22 experienced practitioners from across the country to reflect on equality/inequality – in class, race, gender, poverty, disability and homelessness as well as health and education. They are concerned about individuals as well as ideas and policy instruments. Short and accessible, a pause for thought and inspiration for those concerned with action.

13. Hiding in Plain Sight – Exploring Scotland's ill health | *Carol Craig*
Scotland. A country that prides itself on its modernity and progressive instincts. Yet this is a nation whose mental and physical health outcomes are poor by European standards. This book asks why? Grippingly readable yet challenging, Carol Craig offers an answer which is glaringly obvious. Generations of Scottish children

have suffered in ways that undermine the nation's health. Starting from her own and her neighbours' lives, she explores the growing awareness internationally of the impact of Adverse Childhood Experiences.

14. Right from the Start – Investing in parents and babies | *Alan Sinclair*

Scotland languishes in the second division of global child well-being. One child in every four is judged to be 'vulnerable' when they enter primary school. Alan Sinclair reveals the harm inflicted on so many of our youngest, most defenceless citizens through a toxic mix of poor parenting, bad health and a society focussed on dealing with consequences rather than causes. He also sets out a routemap for us to start putting children first by helping us all to become better parents.

15. The Golden Mean – fostering young people's resilience, confidence and well-being | *Morag Kerr (Editor)*

How do we encourage children and young people and help foster the skills they need to thrive in our increasingly complex world? This insightful and stimulating collection of writings by activists, people who work with the young, commentators and young people themselves provides a compelling answer. We need to strike a healthy balance between support and challenge – 'the golden mean'.

16. The Dear Wild Place | *Emily Cutts*

This book recounts the frenetic campaign to protect a magical oasis in the heart of a busy city from housing development – a David and Goliath struggle. Shows how a grassroots initiative can address the intensive materialism of modern life, improve children's lives, provide precious outdoor space for play and health, build a vibrant community and break down barriers caused by pronounced income inequality. An inspiration to all.

More titles are planned for 2021.
Books can be ordered from www.postcardsfromscotland.co.uk or from www.amazon.co.uk Kindle editions are also available for some titles.

a campaign to introduce a
kindergarten stage
for children aged
three to seven

Follow us on Facebook (Upstart Scotland) or Twitter (@Upstart Scot) www.upstart.scot

Upstart is a Scottish Charitable Incorporated Organisation (SCO47775), run by unpaid volunteers, and financed by donations from supporters and occasional income from training days and conferences.

Membership is free via the website www.upstart.scot
Further information from info@upstart.scot